rich thinking
about the
world's poor

rich thinking about the world's poor

SEEING POVERTY THROUGH GOD'S EYES

Peter Meadows

First published 2003 by Spring Harvest Publishing Division
and Authentic Lifestyle

09 08 07 06 05 04 03   7 6 5 4 3 2 1

Authentic Lifestyle is an imprint of Authentic Media
PO Box 300, Carlisle, Cumbria CA3 0QS
and PO Box 1047, Waynesboro, GA 30830-2047, USA
www.paternoster-publishing.com

British Library Cataloguing in Publication Data

A catalogue record for this book is available from the
British Library

1-85078-518-X

Cover design by Chris Gander
Printed in Great Britain by Bell and Bain Ltd., Glasgow

Contents

Preface

There are three things you deserve to know before reading this book –

1. *This is not one of those 'guilt trip' books*
Picking up a book about 'the poor' can make any sane person nervous. Thumbing through its pages you wait for the ambush – convinced the aim is to heap as much guilt on you as possible. That some deep plot is at work to have you booking your ticket to some remote outpost by the last chapter. Or selling everything you have – and as much of anyone else's that you can get your hands on – to help change the future for those who don't have one.

But not this book. Guilt is an unattractive and, in the long term, an unproductive emotion. These pages have a far higher objective.

2. *This book is for those who already have their eyes open*
There is no shortage of books designed to convince you that the poor are a priority to God, and that we have a responsibility to behave that way too. Though I thank God for them, this book is not one of them. Rather, these pages are for those with their eyes already open to seeing the poor from God's perspective – including those already putting such convictions into practice.

This book is about insight and inspiration. Insight into the rich thinking now increasingly at work among those committed to changing the future of the world's poor, and about inspiring you to understand them, emulate them and support them. And, in some cases to be inspired to go and do likewise.

There was a time when the most those who cared about the poor could manage was to do our best in Jesus' name. To launch forth with a heady cocktail of energy, passion, and sacrifice in the service of the poor. But now there is richer thinking out there – which is what this book is about.

3. *The rich thinking is far from all mine*

I am a new boy on the rich-thinking block. It's true I did play a minor role over twenty-five years ago in helping launch what has become one the UK's largest Christian aid and development agencies. And have championed the cause of the poor ever since. But the past two years or so have opened my eyes to how much I didn't know about what I thought I knew.

Since joining World Vision UK in 2000 it has been like being let loose in an Aladdin's cave. Free to plunder the jewels of a generation of rich thinkers and practitioners. Those who have mostly been too busy thinking and doing to get any of it down on paper in a way that comes alive for those who lack their experience or knowledge.

Which means what follows has a lot to do with me raiding the minds of Christian practitioners who have a vast experience in development. Pioneers like World Vision's Jyakuma Christian, and Bryant Myers – whose deeper writings you'll find listed under the bibliography at the end. And those from the International

Programmes Team at World Vision UK who have patiently led me by the hand through territory they know like the back of theirs.

Credit too goes to my esteemed World Vision colleagues. Particularly Peter Scott who, with his considerable grasp of both theology and the issues of development, has made sure I bumped into the right information at the right time. And gently steered me away from the many elephant traps that await a novice like me when pontificating about the poor. Also to Sarah Coe for all inspired help with much of the research.

Credit must go too to the extensive resources available to me at World Vision where skilled writers and communicators on every continent continue to generate deep wells of high-quality first-hand information in which to dip my creative bucket.

At the same time, I do take the credit for putting my very inquisitive nature to work. Reading, borrowing, foraging, nicking interesting documents from other people's printers at World Vision. But how could I not? This rich thinking stuff is exhilarating territory. At least, it has been for me – and I trust it will be so for you.

Ready? Then please engage brain and turn the page.

Peter Meadows – January 2003

An Introduction

An American philosopher once said, 'Whenever anyone says that he wants to help me, I flee!'

I think that most of us know what he was talking about. So often those who want to help us end up unintentionally hurting us in the process of their so-called 'helpful' ventures. We find ourselves patronised, and even humiliated by people who reach out to us and try to give us what *they* think we need. They fail to see a host of unintentional side effects of their 'good works'.

Some insightful reflections on how our well-meant efforts to live out a God ordained impulse to show compassion to the poor and oppressed in the Third World are desperately needed. We need to be asking ourselves some serious questions when, after an emotional appeal, we join up with some short-term missionary venture that promises us an opportunity to live out the command of Christ to feed the hungry and lift the burdens of the oppressed.

I know of a large church in Florida that accepted the challenge of a pastor in Haiti to build a small hospital and staff it. Using doctors and nurses from the United States, these Americans would, on a rotating basis, provide year-round services to sick Haitian peasants free of charge. In the months that followed, a team of men from the Florida church made several trips to Haiti, and built an attractive and, by Haitian standards, expensive building. It never occurred to these men, as they laid cinder blocks and poured cement, that they were probably doing work that otherwise might have been done by indigenous workers. Not being able to speak the language of Haiti, they had no awareness that the local people considered these well-meaning men from the United States to be interlopers who were stealing their jobs.

The people in the church back in the States went on an ego trip, congratulating themselves on their missionary vision and financial sacrifices. The pastor in Haiti used the project to enhance his efforts to become a potentate in the region. He used the building of the hospital as a means of constructing a local kingdom for himself. Indeed, a lot of ego hungers were fed. But, none of the American philanthropists or short-term missionaries paid any attention to the fact that their new hospital had made it impossible for a couple of Haitian doctors to keep open the small clinic they had set up just three miles up the road.

The Haitian doctors had been charging fees of just a few pennies from each of their patients. Their services were not as good as those of the expatriates from America, but the clinic had been a Haitian venture and an ongoing means for providing dignity for a people who too often feel that what they can do has little or no value compared to what 'those white folks from America' can.

The missionary project, of that well-intentioned church in Florida, ended up by disempowering a group of Haitians in their efforts to meet the needs of their own people. Sadly, that was the real and most long-lasting effect of what was meant to help people in the name of Jesus.

The ugly side effects of good intentions might have been avoided if the people in that Florida church had taken the advice of some folks who had urged them to consult with World Vision or some other experienced mission organisation prior to venturing into an area of ministry about which they had little knowledge.

But the pastor of the church had replied to that suggestion by cynically announcing that he did not trust such big organisations. He preferred to work person to person through the Haitian pastor whom he had come to know during a four-day preaching mission at that pastor's church.

Only after it became obvious that there were problems, did the Florida pastor seek help from World Vision, which put him and his church in contact with indigenous field workers in Haiti who informed them that the particular Haitian pastor with whom they were working had a less than sterling reputation and was known for siphoning off missionary dollars for his own use. These Christians in Florida had to learn the hard way that there is a lot of 'ripping off' by religious con artists in Haiti who have made the manipulation of rich Americans into a profitable   business.

None of this is to say that we should simply stay home and mind our own business, leaving those in the Third World to fend for themselves. In a world wherein wealth is concentrated in the hands of a comparatively few rich nations, it is the responsibility of Christians who have the means of helping the poor to do so. It says in 1 John 3:17,18 that if we have this world's goods, and we know of others who are in desperate need, and we keep what we have while they suffer, we have little right to say that we have the love of God in our hearts.

Through this book, Peter Meadows speaks to those of us who represent 6 per cent of the world's population yet consume 43 per cent of the world's resources. This book is an attempt to get us to ask the right questions about ourselves and our motivations. It asks the strategic questions that must be answered if we are going to do more good than harm in our ministries to the poor.

We have got to get over the arrogance that has hurt so much of the missionary work that we have done in the name of Jesus, and learn to partner with, rather than dominate, those whom we want to help. Ideally, we must learn to serve the poor in the Third World in such a way that, in the end, the indigenous people will say, 'We did it ourselves!'

Tony Campolo
Professor Emeritus
Eastern University
St Davids, PA, USA

1 'Poppie, I am sorry. It was theft'

Her name was Poppie – a bright young girl helping the Ugandan family in whose humble village home I was a guest. She seemed to spend endless hours fetching water from the village borehole. And helping prepare food and cook it over a wood fire in an area between the cabbage patch and the back door.

But what caught my eye, even more than Poppie's bright smile and servant heart, was she did it all wearing a Ralph Lauren designer top. Something that would cost the serious side of £25 in the UK and be much prized by my kids. Of course, she had no idea of the riches on her back. So I told her and watched her bright eyes grow even wider.

To Poppie it was just another top bought with a few Ugandan shillings – the equivalent of UK small change. How this had happened was no mystery. African markets seem full of such items – dumped due to being last year's range or beyond their sell-by date. Which explains the proliferation of Elton John World Tour 1998 and Euro 2000 and the like incongruously adorning backs across the continent.

All well and good. But not for long. On the final day of my visit I looked up to see Poppie with a neatly folded bundle in her hands. Her Ralph Lauren top. 'Please would you take this as a gift for your children?' she offered. And I was about to get it wrong – in spades.

Come on now. I was the one here to do good. To be the hero. To make the sacrifices. To extend my benevolent generosity. But I had been caught on the back foot. There was no script for this – and, forced to ad lib, I blew my lines.

'Oh Poppie, thank you. But no. You need it far more than they do. Thank you. But you keep it.' In my mind was the fact that my kids had 'everything' and it would take her weeks to scrape up even the few pence for a replacement. But I was so wrong, wrong, wrong! Never have I seen a face move from beaming to crestfallen with such swiftness.

How long Poppie had agonised about offering this sacrifice I can only imagine. But this was her way of showing gratitude for my somewhat meagre contribution to her community. It was her opportunity to be the hero – and I had stolen it from her. And there was no way back.

That simple incident will haunt me for ever. It is a challenge to all we may seek to do with those who are poor. How often do those who work among poor communities consign them to being passive 'grateful-or-else' recipients of our own self-promoting kindness? How little do we earnestly seek ways in which they can be the heroes?

How often do we steal from the Poppies of this world their opportunity to behave as though they are rich – with something to offer us?

'Poppie, I am sorry! Through your own act of selfless generosity you taught me one of life's greatest lessons. Something far more valuable than even your Ralph Lauren top. Thank you.'

2 It matters why you think they are poor

Ever wondered why some people fight poverty with education, others with evangelism and others with campaigns for greater justice? Why different groups looking at the same needs come up with different and, at times, even conflicting solutions?

Is it simply horses for courses? Or down to what people personally feel most passionate about? My conviction is there's something far more fundamental going on. That it's all to do with the reason we have for the poor being poor. With the outcome not always in their best interest.

So let me ask you a question. 'Why do you think the poor are poor?' Or, to put it another way, 'What do you see as the great overarching factor that's at the root of poverty?' Your answer matters because it is going to influence the way you respond. Let me illustrate.

Do you see the primary reason for people being poor as due to the fact that they are sinners? That they have never come to a living faith in the one true God and so are not 'experiencing God's blessing' or 'the benefits from righteous living'? If that's your conviction your priority will be evangelism and that's where your energy, money and prayers go.

But what if your view is they are more sinned against than sinners? Then you'll put your emphasis and resources on campaigning for social justice. You will harangue governments to repent rather than individuals.

This stark contrast alone can be seen in the way agencies – and churches – working with the poor select their priorities. One need. Two conclusions. And therefore two very different outcomes. But that's not all. There are other conclusions people make about why there is poverty – and distinct responses that stem from them.

Those who see ignorance as poverty's prime cause put their energy into providing education. Those who see it as all down to the prevailing culture will set about changing it to become just like their own. While, if you see their social system as the culprit, politics are what's used to set about changing things.

Of course, not everyone sees things in such black and white terms. For many, poverty is due to a range of factors rather than just one. Yet even then the range that they go for will impact the kind of response they make. But is even that kind of spread-bet analysis sound enough?

After all, aren't *all* these causes true? Doesn't poverty almost always have to do with human sinfulness *and* the poor being sinned against *and* ignorance *and* aspects of the prevailing culture *and* a flawed social system?

Which means ignoring any one of them is the first step to failing to address the real issues at the heart of a poor community. More than that, the key to bringing change that lasts is to identify and tackle all the issues

– material, medical, social, political, structural and spiritual. And also the complex relationships between them.

Only then will we truly be bringing good news to the poor.

3 For us, for them or for . . .?

Why should plane loads of government ministers be allowed to spend large amounts of our money zipping round the world 'solving' the problems of poverty stricken continents? Particularly when our train service is a shambles, our health service is at the point of collapse and our streets grow ever more dangerous?

Why aren't they giving their time and our money to something far more pressing and important than the world's poor?

Faced with such a question – from a Radio 4 rottweiler – the answer was bazooka-d back by such a government minister. And was delivered with an almost 'how can you be so dumb as not to understand' tone. The reply? Because it's all in our own best interest. Because unless things change in these unstable and poverty ridden nations we will pay the price.

The motivation, then, for acting on behalf of the poor is to make sure fallout from their poverty doesn't rain on our parade. Damage to the environment, economic ruin and increased terrorism all have our name on them unless we act by reducing the levels of poverty out there.

So we ought to care for the poor, we are told, out of our own self-interest. Or should we?

Where does good old compassion and concern for justice come in? Shouldn't there be far higher motives than our own self-interest that drive us? Ought we not to be spurred on by knowing that behind the seemingly endless barrage of horrific statistics are people who simply should not be left to live like this? It is unjust, and unfair.

But are even these motives high enough? Let me suggest they are not. That, worthy as it may be to love my neighbour and stand with them in their poverty, there is something more. And this 'something' is the person and character of God himself.

After all, shouldn't the vision I have for the needs of others essentially have its roots not in the nature of the poor but in the nature of God himself? In who he is, what he likes and – particularly – what lines up with his character?

And he, as trinity, is committed to harmonious relationships. He, as the great judge, longs for justice to be shown. He, as love, longs for love that expresses his character to be demonstrated. He, who became incarnate in our world, looks to continue his incarnation through us – as we become incarnate in the world of others.

Or to put it another way, if I get up in the morning with a desire to put a smile on the face of someone, whose face is it? Mine – because of my self-interest, the poor's – out of pity and a sense of responsibility, or God's – because the greatest desire of my heart is to please him?

The problem is that if I am driven to meet the needs of a hurting world out of my own self-interest I can switch off when enough has been done to keep harm at bay.

And if my motivation is the poor themselves then how long before compassion fatigue takes its toll?

Yet if I can capture a glorious and all embracing vision of the magnificent God of creation and redemption – his character and his purposes – how can I not be motivated forever to live and act in ways that please him.

So, when it comes to 'who's it for', for me it's no contest. Of course, it is too much to expect a government to see it this way. But at least we can. Can't we?

4 Did Jesus ever ask a stranger question?

Most likely you know the incident well. Face to face with Jesus comes Bartimaeus, a begging blind man who, moments earlier, was desperately and incessantly appealing for his help. And now Jesus inexplicably asks him the strangest question, 'What do you want me to do for you?' (Mark 10:51).

Even for someone who was not God in human form this had to be, if you will excuse the pun, blindingly obvious. And for someone who was, the question is even harder to explain. Wasn't it plain, staring-you-in-the-face apparent? Add the fact that Jesus was 'leaving the city' (v. 46), with his work there done and dusted, and you are bound to wonder why he didn't just get on with it and heal him.

But wrap your mind round what was going on and you'll have to admit that the answer is magnificent. Stunningly and awe-inspiringly magnificent. It's a case of the powerful giving the powerless the supreme dignity of choice. And the absolute right to decide his own future.

In case you have just let one of the great truths of what it means to serve the poor rush past you I am going to say it again – because it is simply too good to miss. Take a deep breath and let it soak in. It is about the one who has all the power – Jesus – giving the one who is totally powerless – a blind beggar – the supreme dignity and right to choose his own future.

Bartimaeus will have to live with the consequences of his decision and these are going to be significant. In the days ahead, when life is far more complicated and demanding than just sitting passively by the roadside receiving hand outs, he has to know it was his decision that gave him a very different future. Or to put it an-other way and into a far wider context, what people ask for themselves they are more likely to 'own' and take responsibility for.

Let me throw in a little illustration to show what I mean, with some of the details changed to protect the 'guilty'. The affluent church in a large suburb of

⁴⁶Then they came to Jericho. As Jesus and his disciples, together with a large crowd, were leaving the city, a blind man, Bartimaeus (that is, the Son of Timaeus), was sitting by the roadside begging.

⁴⁷When he heard that it was Jesus of Nazareth, he began to shout, 'Jesus, Son of David, have mercy on me!'

⁴⁸Many rebuked him and told him to be quiet, but he shouted all the more, 'Son of David, have mercy on me!'

⁴⁹Jesus stopped and said, 'Call him.' So they called to the blind man, 'Cheer up! On your feet! He's calling you.' ⁵⁰Throwing his cloak aside, he jumped to his feet and came to Jesus.

⁵¹'What do you want me to do for you?' Jesus asked him.

The blind man said, 'Rabbi, I want to see.'

⁵²'Go,' said Jesus, 'your faith has healed you.' Immediately he received his sight and followed Jesus along the road.

(Mark 10:46-52)

a western city became aware of a poor community on another continent. How is not important. What happened next is.

With no thought of asking 'the Bartimaeus question' the powerful made their own judgement as to what should be gratefully received – with an offer to build a school.

The building was eventually completed. With the powerless expressing their dutiful gratitude and the powerful glowing with pride. And all was well until the moment of reality finally arrived – when the church received the message 'the roof of your school is leaking. Please come and mend it'.

Jesus' seemingly inexplicable question also points to the danger of assuming we always know what's best for the lives of others. Tell the poor what you plan to do for them and the answer will almost certainly be 'thank you' – because it always is, even if they have far greater needs. They know better than to try to negotiate and so risk ending up with nothing.

Let me illustrate once more – with the details again mangled for the same reason as before. The development agency looked at the lack of education on offer for the village and said, 'let us build you a school'. But when they did, few children attended – because they were needed in the fields to supplement the income of their poor families. Had the agency – sincere, dedicated and hard working as they were – stopped to ask 'the Bartimaeus question' they would have first worked to improve the crop yield.

Obvious isn't it? And when it comes to our own response to a world in need - be it as those who 'do' or those who 'give' – it's an answer we dare not miss. Those in a position to play 'God' in people's lives need to act like him.

And don't let it miss your attention that the end result for Bartimaeus was he 'followed Jesus along the road' (v. 52). Ask the right questions and make the right response and that's also more likely to be the outcome.

Population – the facts

- The world's population increases by 200 people every minute.
- Some 73 million people are added to the world's population every year.
- World population grew by 600 million in the nineteenth century and by 4.4 billion in the twentieth century.
- More than 95 per cent of the world's population growth is taking place in the developing world.

5 How to do 'good' and make the poor even poorer

Cows in the little English village of Axbridge, Somerset, have been refusing to cross yellow lines painted on the road as part of the traffic control system. The theory? That the animals think the lines are a cattle grid – with the result that the farmer has to take them on a cross country route to reach their destination.

It reminds me of the ex-prison inmate who always flinched when reaching for a door handle – because those that had been off limits while he was inside had been rigged with a slight electric charge.

What has all this got to do with the price of tea in China or, far more relevantly, with changing the future for the poor? Glad you asked. And the answer is it has nothing at all to do with the going rate for a cup of steaming Lapsang Souchong but everything to do with working with the poor.

The issue here is 'conditioning' and what people come to consider as true – and which then impacts the way they think and behave. Let me illustrate. Please picture yourself treated as an object of pity. As someone viewed as though they are trapped, hopeless and helpless. With no prospect of a better future – unless some benevolent 'hero' comes to rescue you. Got it?

That is your lens of reality – your yellow line on the road or tingly doorknob – that will shape your attitude and behaviour.

Now change the lens completely. Allow yourself to be seen not as hopeless and helpless but as intelligent, diligent, resourceful and hard working. Yes, you are still desperately lacking life's essentials. But the reason you have remained that way is simply because you lack the opportunity or the means to change the way things are.

Seen from this new perspective you are still the same person but, already, you are 'richer' – simply because of the way others see you and, therefore, treat you. Now, no longer perceived as an object of helpless pity, you stand taller; have a greater sense of self-worth.

That's why the attitude of those working with the poor – or providing the resources to make this work happen – is fundamental. Because, even in doing good, we can inflict harm – by reinforcing the wrong perception poor people may have of themselves or the way others see them.

And it is not about pretending something's true that isn't. About kidding the poor and ourselves that, though they really have nothing to offer, we will act as though they have. We're *nice* people! We will change the label on the box despite what is inside – with the aim that the poor will at least get to feel a bit better about themselves despite having no good reason to do so.

It is not like that because, in reality, if the poor really were lacking in intelligence, diligence, resourcefulness and a willingness to work hard, they would never have survived this long. Nor would there be such stunning evidence of what they can do given the opportunity and resources that have been denied them for so long. Which is why we must work *with* the poor as mutual partners – with both parties regarded as having something of great value to contribute. And not see ourselves as working *for* them – where they are little more than hopeless and helpless recipients of our benevolent superiority.

The role of those who serve the poor is to do more than change their circumstances. It's also to enhance their sense of self-worth. To help each individual see themselves as made in God's image – and having all the self-esteem and potential this implies.

After all, they are poor enough already without us robbing them of their dignity too.

6 It's a complex issue, the edifice complex

When it comes to responding to poverty there are some seemingly simple no-brainers. And mostly they involve bunging up a building. An orphanage or two, a school or three. A hospital or six.

There's a need, so let's build something. But is this always the best we can do when addressing need? To send forth or fund a plethora of builders in Jesus' name! All the while imagining we have done our best! There are big issues here, for those who cough up the money, those who put it to use and those on the receiving end.

For a start, how often is our thinking conditioned by what donors are the most willing to pay for rather than what poor communities need and want? Let's face it, buildings are solid and tangible things you can photograph, visit, declare open and produce detailed plans for. They are also things we understand because we have them ourselves.

In contrast, you can't photograph a range of newly acquired skills, strategies or abilities. Or stick a plaque with your name on a community's increased ability to care for the most needy among them, to better negotiate with their landlords or local civil authorities for improved conditions, or to resolve longstanding conflicts with their neighbours that are hindering their progress.

But a permanent, tangible, photographable and visitable edifice to our generosity is something different. It's something about which we can say 'we did that' – with pride.

Second, buildings are an easy, hardly-worth-a-second-thought solution. Education, healthcare, the care of orphans and those with special needs all need a roof over their head. Don't they?

As you struggle to say something other than 'of course' consider what painful experience in Cambodia over the past two decades has to say to us on the subject. When domestic unrest comes – and it's on the increase in our world – what enduring value do walls and roofs offer when they collapse under bombs and tanks or when the people scatter for their lives?

Just suppose the same money, time and effort had been poured into giving the community knowledge, know-how, networks of skilled relationships and so on? Then there would have been something to sustain those in need wherever they were, buildings or not. Then they would have something no invaders could render worthless.

But what about orphanages? Are they the best idea? Or even a good one? In some communities parents who are poor, though perfectly able to care for their young, willingly give away their children to be brought up under such a roof. For them it is the most loving thing to do. Which means there's an inexhaustible supply of children waiting for the orphanages we in the west just love to build and then have to go on funding year on year on year.

There's a better way, as agencies like World Vision have come to realise. It's to commit the same level of expenditure and expertise into helping the poor community enrich their lives to a level where they can care for their own.

In some settings even a school is not the best way to go. Take the community that said 'yes' to a school but left it almost empty of pupils when the opening ceremony was over, the bunting had been put away and the two hours of speeches had finally come to an end. Why? Because the local economy forced the children to be an essential part of the workforce. Without them sharing in working in the fields neither they nor their families would have had enough to eat.

Better than four walls and a roof would have been to spend the same money and effort on something un-photographable – like better seeds, alternative crops, training in more productive methods. All the while making informal education available out of working hours.

Of course there are exceptions to the 'don't build it' approach. There has to be a place for schools, hospitals, and special care homes – at the right time and in the right place. But this is no reason to park our brains and failing to ask whether all the buildings we in the west, and in the church, fund and erect are genuine 'exceptions'. Or if too many are simply the result of shallow short-term, heart-jerk, thinking – with a dose of western imperialism and our own edifice complex thrown in?

Indeed, will the day ever come when a UK church says, 'We are planning our own building project and would like to match the money we raise by supporting something in a poor community. Something like increasing the leadership and decision-making skills of the community's leaders' – I dream about it.

7 A before and after story – that left the media cold

When religion and newspaper headlines collide it is seldom good news. It's more likely to be about scandal, controversy or human failure. Which means most people could easily imagine that nothing life-enhancing was ever the result of having a faith in God.

We are good for our jumble sales, the usual round of hatching, matching and dispatching. But we are about as valuable to real life as a soup spoon with holes.

If only the media would look a little deeper – like at the ten-year community development project that, not that long ago, came to an end among twelve poor villages in Gummidipoondi, about thirty miles north of Madras, India. What happened in that seemingly hopeless situation, through the influence of Christians committed to the needs of those who are poor, reveals an amazing before and after story that deserved the headline news it never got.

Before, for the villagers it was an eight-mile journey to get even basic medicines. Now, health workers have them on hand. Before, sick people were taken to the local temple priest, who invoked the spirits to try to heal them. Now there is a doctor for people to go to.

Before, giving birth was a far from safe experience as the result of the superstitious and unwise traditional practices of the village. Now, mothers can give birth under safe and hygienic conditions. Before, pregnancies just 'happened' – with an often-disastrous impact on the ability of their parents to cope with the economic consequences. Now people understand the importance of having fewer and healthier children – and what's involved for that to happen.

Before, work was scarce. Now, the project runs a thriving tailoring centre offering training and employment. And financial help has been given to families so they can start their own small businesses.

Before, the village people were too timid to confront the police or government officials in pursuit of their rights and fought for their share of the resources. Now they are able to express themselves without fear, having formed themselves into organisations and been given

And here's some more good news

It is not only in villages that good things are happening. In a world overstocked with doom and gloom here's something more to put a smile on your face.

- *Over the past 30 years, the developing world has halved the number of infant deaths.*
- *In the past 30 years, 63 countries have reduced eaths of children under five by one-third. A further 100 countries reduced under-five mortality by one-fifth.*
- *Over the past 10 years, deaths of yung children from diarrhoea-based diseases were reduced by half – saving 1.5 million lives each year.*
- *The increse in the numbers of children going to school is outpacing population growth, so that more children are in school now than ever before.*
- *Worldwide, the number of major armed conflicts – almost all internal – declined from 55 in 992 to 36 in 1998.*
- *By 1975, only 33 countries has ratified the International Covenant on Civil and Political Rights; by 2000, 144 had done so.*

training in how to speak up for themselves. The women have even registered themselves under the Societies Act to tap government resources.

This has led to the creation of community centres that provide classes in the evenings for children, somewhere for community leaders to discuss day-to-day issues, and a place where the women can share their joys and sorrows with one another.

Before, the people did not understand about the dangers of alcohol, tobacco and casual sex. Now they do and are changing the way they behave.

Before, there were no churches in the area and widespread ignorance of the Christian faith. Now there are churches in all twelve villages.

There's only one word for it – 'transformation'. It happened because just a few people heard and obeyed God's call to go, to love and to act. And because others sacrificed to make it possible through their gifts and prayers.

The fact that it was a World Vision project is immaterial. But what is, is the fact that this amazing transformation didn't grab even an inch of the headlines or a second of the TV news because this isn't the kind of sensational religious story that gets covered. Perhaps one day?

8 But who gets the credit? Us or our God?

In the sophisticated west it's hard to imagine a world that believes life is still subject to magic. Sure, we do live in a society rife with superstition and where more than a few have been bamboozled into thinking that David Blaine and the like have something more going for them than 100 per cent trickery. But that's not what I mean.

Instead, picture a community where, almost to a person, they believe the answer to life is to find the most powerful god and keep him on your side. A community where simple scientific acts like finding water or growing healthy crops have 'gods' – with personality and 'feelings' at their heart.

And such a world most definitely exists. It's a world Christian development agencies encounter every day. And how they handle it makes a crucial difference to the way those they serve understand *why* they do what they do – and *who* they do it for.

Picture about thirty villagers standing under a baobab tree in northern Senegal. They're watching a World Vision soil scientist and a hydrologist working on the best site for a new borehole. The scientist is taking soil samples and his colleague is studying a hydrological survey spread over the bonnet of their car.

Of course, you understand perfectly what's going on. But what about those villagers? Chasing an answer you turn to your imaginary translator, *'What do you folks think these people are doing?'*

Comes the reply, *'That's simple. They are witch doctors. The one in the dirt is asking the spirit of the earth where the spirit of the water is. And the other one's consulting sacred texts, written in a secret language, just like our mullahs do.'*

'Are they any good?' you ask in shock. *'Oh, yes. They are better than our witch doctors. They always find the water.'* And they will.

You, the soil scientist and hydrologist are clear. The water was found by western science. But the locals explain the miracle of finding water though the lens of their traditional worldview. To them it must be magic, because there is no other rational explanation.

It was a chillingly bad moment when a Christian development agency found a village in India had added a further deity to their list of gods – complete with a shrine. It was chillingly bad because this new deity was them.

So what should the Christian agency say to the villagers in situations like this? If it is not magic, what is it? Say 'only science' and we contribute to the secularisation of their worldview. We move them towards a belief that only the physical and rational are real. But say nothing and we further reinforce their traditional worldview, leaving them to continue in their superstition. Neither is a Christian thing to do.

So what explanation can be truly Christian? The 'im-aginary' situation above was actually the genuine experience of Bryant Myers, a World Vision Vice President. And it was he who first raised this issue in my mind.

I like Bryant's answer, though it may not always be easy to express or to have it believed. It's that the true God created a rational material universe. He also created us – those who come in Jesus' name to work alongside the poor – in his image. And therefore made us able to figure out how his world works and the natural rules it follows.

Such an explanation allows God to be God and also validates science as his creation. Fail to understand the need to explain things that way and we may not be being as Christian as we think we are. Or as Christian as we need to be.

9 Heroes get younger every day

Who are your heroes? Mother Teresa? Martin Luther King? Some of mine are somewhat younger – like Eder Contreras. Who at only eleven years old became President of the board of directors of the Children Peace Builders Movement in war-torn Colombia. Yes – at eleven.

Unlike Moses, who didn't get 'the big job' until he was about eighty, Eder was not willing to hang about that long to do his bit for justice and change. And nor was Mayerly Sanchez. At the much riper age of fourteen she became one of three girls nominated for the 1998 Nobel Peace Prize for their leadership in Colombia's Mandate for Peace, Freedom and Life, a UNICEF grassroots children's movement.

Don't underestimate the challenge Mayerly and her cohorts are facing. For more than twenty years drug-fuelled conflict has raged in Colombia. Today, conflict is a way of life in eight of Colombia's 32 departments, affecting one in five of the total population and claiming over 40,000 lives since 1990. Children make up about 65 per cent of Colombia's internal refugees.

It's in this context that every week, Mayerly would meet with 30 children in her community to learn more about being good peace promoters in their families, schools, and communities. She also discussed legislation with Colombian Congressmen, led university conferences on the peace process, organised rallies, lobbied officials and ran a kids' club on top of her after-school job.

Equally up for starting early is Raquel Puerto Serranos from Nicaragua. Aged only twelve, she was chosen to lead The Forum for Girls and Teenagers that confronts the discrimination girls and young women face in Nicaragua on a daily basis. They are constantly last in line for almost everything including education and protection from sexual harassment and abuse. Raquel has held press conferences and her stories have been published in her national press and on the radio.

For these three heroes – and many like them – age was to be no barrier as they did what they could to change the future for their community. Of course, they couldn't have done it totally by themselves. Help received on the way included all of them being children sponsored through World Vision. They were also given the encouragement and opportunity to stand up and be counted – which is an essential component in World Vision's commitment to giving all who are poor a voice of their own – whatever their age or gender.

The approach is rooted in the example of Jesus, who not only spoke of the importance and value of children but also gave them dignity by the way he treated them. And when you actively do the same the outcome can be stunning – as the examples of Eder, Mayerly and Raquel testify. Then, even an eleven-year-old can become a hero.

Yet there is even more to it than that, because these famous three are but the tip of a very large iceberg. It is because of what is happening on a much wider basis that heroes like this emerge. Which is quite another story – as told elsewhere in this book.

10 If only good news was always good

It looked like any other clump of bamboo huts huddled beside an Asian roadside. But it was nothing of the kind, explained my travelling companion, as we juddered north from Phnom Phen on what, in Cambodia, passes for a road.

This anonymous cluster of bamboo and corrugated iron was the notorious prostitution village of Svay Pak. Here the menu included children as young as ten. Locals and sex-tourists alike came to slake their perverted sexual thirst with just some of the one million new children a year, worldwide, forced to become unwilling participants.

Coming that close brought an unwelcome chill to the hot and humid air. Feeling sick from more than the potholes, we journeyed on. But I have never forgotten the seeming ordinariness of the setting or the horror lurking behind the fragile walls.

But now the welcome news has come. The village, euphemistically known by taxi drivers as 'K11' for being eleven kilometres north of Phnom Penh, is no more. The government swooped bringing it all to an end. Yes, it may well have been a cosmetic exercise a day before the start of a regional tourism conference. After all, the Police Chief did admit it was an effort to salvage Cambodia's cultural reputation. But at least it had happened.

Yet how much good news is it really? Is this yet one more victory for justice and morality? One small but significant step in the fight to protect and defend children at risk? Stifle the cheers. Put the champagne on ice. Tragically, the outcome could well put sexually exploited children at even greater risk. Not because of the end result but due to the speed at which it took place – an overnight swoop that brought a seemingly instant end to an unacceptable situation.

But those who know – and who are not out simply to enhance their reputation – shout with alarm that shutting the brothels in an instant means the trade will simply slink underground, leaving those committed to the welfare of the children no longer able to care for them.

In Svay Pak, for example, World Vision were running daily kids' clubs – helping over two hundred children understand their right not to be sexually exploited and ways to lessen the chance of this happening. Vital work like this, along with the practical healthcare that can go with it, goes out of the window if the children are relocated by their pimps to yet another set of bamboo buildings – who knows where? – disappearing for months or even years.

That's why there is a frightening tightrope to walk. With agencies working flat out to bring this terrible trade to an end. But knowing it has to happen gradually, so that families can find other sources of income and children will have the support of those who can give them a better and healthier future. For those with an absolute view of morality – where wrong is always wrong, and black and white is never grey – this is a hard issue to face. But it is the reality.

At the same time, the motivation to end child prostitution needs to stem from more than the desire for a country to protect its cultural reputation. It's the children at risk who need protection – and it is a double tragedy when what should be good news for them may be nothing of the sort.

Children – the facts

- More than ten million children still die each year from preventable causes. That's 30,000 a day – or one every three seconds.
- One billion lack access to safe drinking water.
- 30 million are not vaccinated against diseases that could be prevented.
- Over 150 million still suffer from malnutrition.
- More than 250 million children have to work so their families can eat.
- 125 million children do not go to school – the majority girls.
- 100 million have been orphaned as the result of HIV/AIDS.
- Every year at least half a million children go partially or totally blind because of vitamin A deficiency.
- 1.2 million girls under 18 are trafficked for prostitution each year – with over 1,000,000 children working in the sex trade in Asia alone.
- Some 300,000 children serve as soldiers in conflicts spanning 50 countries.
- Two million children have been killed and six million permanently injured in conflicts in the past ten years.

11 It's the condom conundrum

For western Christians, who tend to equate the condom with casual sex, the present global AIDS crisis poses a huge dilemma. To condom or not to condom – that's the question. And, in answering it, Christians are not always being 'good news'.

So let's put the issue bluntly, should a Christian agency ever give out condoms? And, if so, in what circumstances?

But first, one indisputable fact. It's that, in the context of a programme of education and awareness raising, the distribution and correct use of condoms helps slow the spread of HIV in poor communities.

However, is it legitimate – in order to save lives – for Christians to encourage something that seems to endorse casual sex? Are there times when the lesser of two evils is the most Christian thing to do? And remember, we are not talking about western sophistication – where the evidence suggests that the more condoms you hand out the worse things can get. This is a very different picture. For example . . .

Meet Greeta – who, in a Zambian border town, sells her body night after night, and day after day, with the truck drivers passing through as her eager customers.

Greeta's one of thousands who see this as the only way to keep their family from starvation. To her it's not a matter of choice but necessity. She isn't responsible for the fact that the crops have failed yet again. And there is no other work. But she does feel responsible for keeping her young family alive – in any way she can.

Tonight she will ply her trade – knowing that unprotected sex pays double. Will you give her a condom – with her future and that of her children in mind? Or take the moral high ground? Controversial as it sounds, the response of a Christian agency like World Vision is to teach women like this how to negotiate protected sex with their customers. And give them the condoms they need to do so.

HIV/AIDS – the story in brief

The HIV epidemic is the most devastating that humanity has ever faced and has become the fourth biggest global killer.

- Worldwide, more than 42 million people are living with AIDS and 20 million have already died.
- More than 14 million have become orphans having lost one or both their parents.
- There are an estimated 14,000 new cases of HIV/AIDS each day.
- Children under the age of fifteen make up 2,000 of the new daily cases of HIV/AIDS.
- Nearly 600,000 children under fifteen die each year from HIV/AIDS.
- In Swaziland, Botswana and some areas of South Africa, more than a third of pregnant women are HIV positive
- The virus will kill more people over the next 10 years than all the wars and disasters of the past fifty.

In sub-Saharan Africa AIDS has wiped out 50 years of progress. Today, life expectancy is only forty-seven years. Without AIDS it would have been sixty-two years. And in some southern African countries up to half of all new mothers could die of AIDS.

And there are other settings that present equal challenges to our understanding of morality. For example, meet Jakob – who made a dreadful mistake while working away from home for six months and is now HIV positive and deeply remorseful. And meet Anna his wife. Will you leave them to their own devices? Or give them one of yours?

Meet Tabbi, Omoko and Lydia. One brutally raped by invading soldiers. One given unscreened blood when the delivery of her last child went wrong. The other, one of thousands waiting to hear the safe sex message that the overwhelmed and under-resourced community health workers in her area will one day have the time to patiently explain. What will you do for them on the condom front? Provide them?

For those who say that to do so 'sounds like saying sin is OK' the question has to be 'So what's your answer?' After all, isn't 'good news' supposed to be good news?

12 'Listen to us' – say the poor. 'Please slow down'

What would the poor say to those working on their behalf, given half a chance? Perhaps that's not a thought to have ever rumbled through your cranium. So now is your moment. What would they say? And to provide the answer you richly deserve I'm going to let Karunawathie Menike tell you. As a peasant leader from north-west Sri Lanka she minces no words – as you are about to discover.

Karunawathie would have us know that programmes to 'empower the poor' and bring swift change can be misguided. Such initiatives, she insists, are too often *'based on the false assumption that we, the poor, do not know how to overcome our poverty and improve our own condition, that we do not have knowledge about the cause of our poverty and how to overcome it: and that we are lethargic and tend to accept our poverty as our fate'*.

Get that. We, those who are working to bring change to poor communities – agencies, churches, governments or whatever – stand accused. Accused of wrongly believing the poor have no idea how to bring change themselves. Accused of treating them as though they are ignorant as to the reasons at the root of them being poor. And, for good measure, accused of seeing them as lazy into the bargain and resigned to the way things are.

But that's not the way it is, this spokesperson for the poor would have us know. Pointing the finger at NGOs (Non Governmental Agencies) and governments themselves, Karunawathie accuses, *'They seem to want to enter our villages to shake us up and wake us from what they think is our slumber and tell us that we must take our future into our own hands to create ways of improving our quality of life.'*

To her this is 'quite hilarious'. Why? Because those who plan the empowerment of the poor *'clearly don't understand our reality, our priorities, our wishes, our thought processes, our constraints, and our needs.'* That's some list.

If they did understand, Karunawathie argues, they would know that the poor have a greater sense of reality regarding the future. It is a sense of reality that's *'not utopian like those removed from the earthly realities of life in poor communities'*. And they would also know that going too fast in the pursuit of progress, in the social, economic, and political systems in which the poor are placed, *'would not only be unrealistic but self-destructive'*.

Karunawathie adds, *'The poor know full well that if they were to empower themselves – which they do – it has to be done very carefully. Act fast in a hostile environment and we could easily trip and fall.'*

Essentially her message is – 'Change must happen at our own pace and not yours.' So why not? The answer is simple – because this presents problems for governments and development agencies alike. They can't hang about. Things need things to happen fast. Because for governments votes can depend on it. And for development agencies that's what donors love to hear. The more they can speak about change and at a pace, the more their supporters are going to be motivated to give again.

So here's the deal. Whose voice is going to get the greatest attention from those working on behalf of the poor? Their donors? The voters? Or the poor themselves – who at times want us to move at their own travelling speed rather than the one that suits us best? OK. Who?

Karunawathie Menike served as Chairperson of the People's Rural Development Association which brings together the business, scientific and professional communities of Sri Lanka with development NGOs and community based organisations to promote employment through small enterprise. Her words are from Development Practice Vol. 3 Number 3 (1993).

13 Even better news than we realise?

How do you feel about those who were once desperately poor becoming magnificently rich? Moving from where they have lacked even life's basic essentials to being genuinely and over-flowingly prosperous? The equivalent in our western culture of being two-car, detached owner-occupiers with enough spare for two weeks at Disney every year, in charge of a workforce to run their factory, and having a leading role in their church.

Are you really sure you feel comfortable – even enthusiastic about the total concept? And committed to seeing it happen? Really, really?

I'm asking because when it comes to being 'good news to the poor' I'm beginning to feel we are significantly short sighted. Not merely blinkered or out of focus. But actually with a severely stunted vision as to what God ultimately has in mind for the 'have nots' of our world.

Be brutally honest with me for a moment, don't we think it's all done and dusted when – to continue quoting from Isaiah – we've bound up the broken-hearted, announced freedom for captives and comforted the mourners? That, with such progress behind us, we think we've done rather well?

It's as though our aim is not much more than to make things a little more tolerable for those in need. To see them lifted up from their own ground zero where life is now bearable and acceptable for them and not guilt inducing for us. But what about the possibility of them actually becoming genuinely and affluently 'rich' and influential? Does that sit comfortably with you? Or is the thought one that creates at least a tinge of discomfort and hesitation?

In which case, please read on in that passage from Isaiah 61, the one Jesus made his manifesto, to discover what God really has in mind. Because as the result of God's good news, those who were once 'poor' are intended to have a whole load more coming their way than we may be dreaming of or working and praying for.

⁴ They will rebuild the ancient ruins
and restore the places long devastated;
they will renew the ruined cities
that have been devastated for generations.
⁵ Aliens will shepherd your flocks;
foreigners will work your fields and vineyards.
⁶ And you will be called priests of the Lord,
you will be named ministers of our God.
You will feed on the wealth of nations,
and in their riches you will boast.
⁷ Instead of their shame
my people will receive a double portion,
and instead of disgrace
they will rejoice in their inheritance;
and so they will inherit a double portion in
*   their land,*
and everlasting joy will be theirs.
(Isaiah 62:4–7)

For a start, they are meant to be achievers in their own right (v. 4). It is *they* who are called to rebuild what was destroyed – relationships, communities, institutions, cities. They are to be the ones who cast their gaze over the end results and gasp 'look what *we* did' rather than 'look what *they* did for us'.

Of course that's the easy bit to stomach because good development practice always has this as its goal. But it is good to be reminded that it's not just good practice, it is also what God has in mind!

However, there is much more that God has in store. Those who were once powerless and servants of others are to come into positions of management, ownership and responsibility (v. 5). It will be *others*, promises Isaiah, who will feed *their* flocks, plough *their* fields and tend *their* vineyards.

Picture what that looks like – which could well be nothing like the dreams we have for the poor. This is not just about poor communities having safe water, adequate healthcare, basic education and such. It's about people taking genuine responsibility for their own lives and communities. Managing not only their own patch but the lives of others as well. And coming to the point where they develop significant businesses that demand employees to do the labouring for them.

They are also to have a special place in their relationship with the living God (v. 6). Can we live with that? Not merely signing up to be pew fodder and passive disciples but 'special' – as 'priests of the Lord' and 'ministers of our God'. Those with a vibrant and vital role to play in the life and future of the church.

And here comes what challenges me most, if I am honest. They are to become more than 'no longer poor', but inheritors of 'a double portion [of prosperity] and everlasting joy' (v. 7). A double portion. Twice what the rest get: 100 per cent more. Those who we all too easily see as needing to have life made a little better are those for whom God has plans stretching way beyond the horizon we have set.

Ownership, significance, influence, responsibility, prosperity, and a special relationship with their Creator

and a role in his church. Are these the dreams we have
for the poor – what we are praying and working for?
They are most definitely on God's mind – so shouldn't
they be on ours too?

14 Just one woman in several million

No one knew her name – but Jesus said she would go down in history. I'm talking about that widow and her mite. Or, perhaps more accurately, the mighty widow (see Luke 21:1–4).

I'm coming to see that there are countless other amazing and almost anonymous individuals who deserve history to record and publish their selfless sacrifice. Those like Sunila, from Sri Lanka, who is symbolic of millions of poor people with the same spirit of sacrifice.

Sunila left school at eleven, joining her father in the paddy field. By the age of sixteen she was already married and living in a small wattle and daub house. And soon there were three children to care for and a husband who worked little and gradually became an alcoholic, spending much of his time in the village pub.

To take care of her children's needs Sunila used to collect all the coconuts from her home garden, husk them and sell the result to buy rice and vegetables. But, as the breadwinner, she knew it would take more than that if she was to provide her children with daily meals, an education and a brick house. So Sunila became a vegetable vendor – collecting various home-grown vegetables, coconuts and fruits to sell on the pavement in the nearest town, about 20 kilometres away.

All the while her husband would come home drunk. Beat her. Chase her out of the house. And even demand her hard-earned money. But Sunila followed her dream, continuing to sell her produce. And, without her husband knowing, putting away a few rupees each week.

It was then that World Vision came to her village, and began running team building meetings for those who wanted to have a better future. Sunila joined a group with seven others – to extend her entrepreneurial skills and learn new ways to develop her family life. She also received a loan from the bank formed by all the small groups, to extend her little business – repaying it within months.

Today Sunila's sixteen-year-old son has completed his education. She's built a brick house and continues with her small business. And her husband, having seen the way things have changed in the home, has stopped drinking alcohol.

Meanwhile, Sunila is still dreaming. Her next task? To construct an oil mill for her son. She has already collected the rocks and sand that will be needed.

Just one woman among a million or more – all working to change the future for themselves and their communities. Individuals who are all too easily overlooked by those who think it is their money or help that matters most. Sure, such support is part of the picture. But not as big a part as we may think.

Without people like Sunila not much would be happening out there. So the least we can do is give her a name check and the credit. And thank God for the millions like her.

15 Can big ever be beautiful?

We live in a world where globalisation is now mostly seen as 'nasty'. Where ubiquitous entities like McDonald's are increasingly regarded as 'the enemy'. By those who riot, those who have no more than a feeling of inward discomfort that big is bad, and growing numbers in between.

In contrast, that which is small and lean - be it the corner shop or a mini co-operative – is generally touted as the most virtuous. All of which leaves me wondering – 'can big ever genuinely be beautiful when it comes to working with the poor?'

And it matters. At least it does to me – because I am just one of the 12,000 people working worldwide for a major development and aid agency. An agency with independent offices in over ninety nations, presently helping some 75 million people, and generating over £500 million in cash and goods to do so each year.

That's big. In fact there are few bigger. But is it genuinely good news to be that big? Is there anything such a humongous juggernaut can really do better than a myriad of smaller agencies each with a minimum of bureaucracy and a nifty turning circle? I have come to believe that there is.

For a start there are the advantages that ought to be just too obvious to overlook – but may well be. Like being able to use what's learned in one project (in fact, every project) to improve the effectiveness of all the others. Like the savings in administration and management costs that come from establishing central administration for common tasks – that mean you can do more with the money you receive.

Like being able to add to your payroll some of the foremost experts in their field – using their outstanding wisdom and experience in order to serve the whole organisation and, thus, the poor. Like being able to establish common standards and values across every programme so as to excel.

Things like this, which ought to be staring-us-in-the-face stuff, deserve to be credited and acclaimed in the context of the 'small is beautiful' assumptions that seem to be growing apace. But there are far bigger issues than these.

First, it is possible to be united against common global enemies – like HIV/AIDS. It takes a mega partnership to make a commitment, as World Vision has done, to raise and spend over £20 million in a united global initiative to reduce infection, suffering and death caused by HIV/AIDS. And then draw on the most expert advice, create the most effective response – and make sure this is implemented in every one of thousands of programmes.

Second, the bigger you are the more loudly you can speak for those with no voice – like the world's children. I'll spare you the horrifying stats on forced child labour, sexual exploitation and the like. But World Vision's united campaign, Imagine a World

Where Children are Safe – with its devastating reports and hard hitting recommendations – has gone to the heart of the UN. Something that would be impossible to achieve by a myriad of small but beautiful agencies.

Third, being big gives you the resources to do essential research into what is not always apparent in the world of the poor – and to put what has been learned to work globally. Which is what World Vision has been able to do on things like the exploitation of children, the neglect of those who are handicapped and the issue of women and violence.

Now before a whole bunch of two men and their dog outfits come beating on my door in protest at having been written off, let me make it clear that this is not what I am saying. Small can be, and is often, very beautiful indeed when it comes to working with the poor. Out there are zillions of initiatives with a sharp focus, a small highly dedicated and motivated team and a glorious lack of bureaucracy, that are helping to change the world. Cheer for them, pray for them, honour them, sell your house for them. And also for the many magnificent middle-size agencies too. But don't assume this is the whole picture.

True, I would always prefer to get my hamburger from the independent Ed's Diner than from Ronald's arches. But sometimes – and this time – let's hear it for the big guy.

16 People are dying of politics

Sir Bob Geldof said it so eloquently. 'People in Africa are not dying of drought, they are dying of politics.' Exactly so. Human decisions in the political arena can have devastating effects. And this fundamental reality is true not only on huge, visible, and well-publicised issues – like trade sanctions and land rights. It's also the way it is in ways that are far less obvious.

For example, when NATO welcomes a new member state into its corporate 'peacekeeping' family, the deal includes the newcomer having to upgrade their arsenal. This has pressured some countries to dump weapons deemed past their 'sell-by date' at bargain prices on the world market.

The result is an abundance of small arms available to some of the poorest nations – and their young. Which is one of the reasons why 300,000 children under eighteen are fighting in many of the world's 37 armed conflicts, with at least one in three soldiers being children aged less than fifteen.

And when the United States introduced legislation aimed at those who use children in exploited labour situations it had an unexpectedly devastating effect. The goal was laudable: to see thousands of children freed from long days of hazardous, mind-numbing, and backbreaking work. The unanticipated result? An estimated 30,000 children, turfed out of the Bangladesh garment industry by employees desperate to keep on the right side of the US.

Wasn't that a great result? Sadly no. Because these children had no choice but to go looking for alternative ways to earn the few pence a day their lives depended on. And then found the only choice was between the safe havens of welding – with no protective clothing – and the sex industry, with its daily risk to their lives. Hooray for the politicians.

- *In 2000 the UK government approved nearly 700 export licences for £64 million worth of weapons and equipment to India and Pakistan.*
- *The 48 LDC's (less developed countries) are the poorest countries in the world. Together they make up a mere 0.4 per cent of world trade.*
- *The energy used by the 45,000 delegates at the 2002 Earth Summit was enough to power one billion kettles or a town of 55,000 Africans for a year.*

It is situations like this – and there are many more – that demand a responsible and realistic response to people in pain. One that includes painting accurate pictures in the minds of those with the power to bring change. And making sure we do our best to see that the political decisions they make really are for the best.

Africa – some facts

- Up to half of Africa's population now lives on less than $1 a day.
- Of the 49 least developed countries (LDCs), described as the poorest of the world's poor, 37 are African.
- Angola provided seven per cent of the US's oil in 2001 – yet one in three of its children die before the age of five.
- Average life expectancy in Mozambique is now under 40 years. The government spends just $2 per person per year on public health.

17 If it's worth doing, do it right

My dad drilled it into me big time: 'If something's worth doing, it's worth doing right.' That's what I heard from as early as I can remember. And it counted for everything from sweeping the kitchen floor to my school assignments.

Those words of great advice still ring in my ears – and have shaped much of my life. But how does his 'doing it right' principle apply to working with poor communities as they transform their future? We understand the need for passion, sincerity, expertise, and money. But what goes into 'doing it right' so far as the poor are concerned?

I've been listening and learning from those who know; who do it right day in and day out. Those committed to seeing the poorest communities eventually standing on their own feet, with the process of development going to go on long after they themselves have moved away. More than that, as followers of Jesus, 'doing it right' for them means doing it as close to 'his way' as they can understand.

I have been drinking deeply at their wells of wisdom, and discovered that those who 'do it right' are convinced that if you want to make a lasting difference in the lives of the poor you must give serious attention to the way you do what you do. There's a name for this 'doing it right' approach. It can all be summed up in the descriptive phrase 'Christ-centred holistic and sustainable development'.

And, to 'do it right', those who know would tell you that you need to:

1. Arrive as a servant – not as a saviour. Think 'feet washing', not 'order giving'.
2. Recognise that God was there before you were and is already at work in the community.
3. Start by listening – because you have more to learn from them than they have from you.
4. Recognise it is only opportunity and resources the poor lack.
5. Help them dream dreams of a different future – and to believe they can do something themselves to bring it about.
6. Help them identify what they can do for themselves – and help them to do it and to get the credit for it.
7. Make sure the programme of action is owned by them and not by you. And that you respond to their decisions rather than imposing yours.
8. Don't treat problems in isolation. Instead, help them identify the needs of their community as a whole – by looking for the links between issues and for the underlying causes of their poverty.
9. Live lives among them that provoke questions about your God – and be ready to answer them.
10. Make sure the deity that receives the credit for the transformation that takes place is not you.
11. When it is time to leave, trust that they will say, 'look what we did'. And make sure you are extra happy if

they hardly notice the role you played. Because that's the way it is supposed to be.

12. Know that just as God was there before you arrived he will continue to be there after you have left.

That's 'doing it right'. And though it may all sound simple, behind each of those twelve points lies a wealth and depth that deserves exploring and applying. Because 'doing it right' makes it 'worth doing' – with all the strength God gives you.

18 If not for our prayers

What possible link could there be between IVF treatment for infertility and the crying needs of poor people the world over? The answer is 'prayer'. Stick with me!

It's a fact that women having fertility treatment are twice as likely to become pregnant if people are praying they'll succeed. Robust research conducted at Columbia University, New York, and published in the respected *Journal of Reproductive Medicine* says so.

It's not even marginal. Researchers put 219 women undergoing IVF treatment into two groups – with half prayed for without them knowing. The scientist expected prayer to have no effect – which is what they were out to prove. Surprise, surprise. Over twice as many from the prayed-for group became pregnant (46 per cent compared with 22 per cent).

A fluke? Not according to other equally significant scientific research.

A study of 990 heart patients published in the *Archives of Internal Medicine* (25.10.99) showed those with someone praying for them suffered fewer complications.

This research took place at the Mid America Heart Institute of St Luke's Hospital in Kansas City. Patients were randomly divided into two groups. One group was prayed for daily by community volunteers who asked for 'a speedy recovery with no complications'. It was a blind trial: none of the patients knew.

After just four weeks the result was striking: the prayed-for patients had suffered ten per cent fewer complications, ranging from chest pain to full-blown cardiac arrest.

A similar study in 1988 at San Francisco General Hospital concluded those not prayed for 'required ventilatory assistance, antibiotics, and diuretics more frequently than patients in the [prayer] group'.

One of the team involved with the IVF research, Prof Rogerio Lobo, said, 'The findings suggest the inclusion of prayer in the treatment protocol may provide a significant impact upon the success of IVF.'

In other words, prayer makes a genuine difference. Which offers great encouragement to all of us who, at times, feel our prayers are like whistling in the wind. In the face of immense human suffering we pray and nothing seems to happen.

Unlike the research involving those longed-for pregnancies and heart problems we can't measure the impact of our prayers. But in the light of the measuring that has been done, who dares think what our world might be like without them? I am encouraged.

19 The cry for justice – or the cries of the poor?

The facts are true. But no names have been used – to protect the poor. Because this situation, like many others in the world of development, is knife-edge stuff.

Some things in this telling scenario can't be disputed. This country's military dictatorship has been charged by the UN with 'crimes against humanity'. They refuse to hand over power to those who have been democratically elected. And there are abiding accusations of the use of child workers and forced labour.

It's a situation that's led many in the developed world be become outraged and to cry for justice. As a result, with the aim of forcing change from within this nation, they have demanded boycotts from without, both from the business world and agencies who bring aid and development.

But there's more to it than that – as is so often the case when dealing with issues of injustice and poverty. This is also one of the poorest countries in the world. Children die often and young. Widespread malnutrition takes its toll. Much of the national infrastructure lies in ruins.

So what do you do when you are a Christian development agency called to serve the poor – whoever they are and wherever they are, including in countries like this? Are you to listen to the cries for 'justice' and throw up your hands in horror? Or listen to the cries of the poor – and get your hands dirty on their behalf. And wrists slapped by those yelling for justice at the same time?

This is not exactly the same question the world of multinational business has been asking about the same country. But it has chilling parallels. And some of the biggest business entities have given their answer by pulling out – not entirely voluntarily – but mostly as the result of concerted lobbying and threatened boycotts of their products from those demanding justice.

But what has been the result of major companies responding to the call to boycott the nation until it has cleaned up its act? One such company had been giving desperately needed employment to 1,000 workers. More than that, the factory they worked in was built to European standards, and the workers did 48 hours a week for above average pay. They even had paid holidays and sick leave.

But no more. The outrage of those publicly calling for change in the way the nation is governed forced the company to pull out. The factory was closed, ending all that the 1,000 workers and their families had enjoyed by way of income, security, good working conditions and benefits.

There are those who see this downside as a means that will eventually justify an end. And they also believe aid and development agencies must join the boycott, even if the poor get hurt in the short term. They deserve to be respected for their sincerely held beliefs – which will have been reached not without a lot of painful reflection.

But I hope they too will respect the equally sincere beliefs of those who have reached a different conclusion. Who, like World Vision for example, have heard both the cries for justice and the cries of the poor – especially the children. And gone for the slapped wrist alternative.

20 Why me, Lord, why me?

At the time I first wrote the following words some five million people – men, women, children – lingered on the edge of starvation in and around Afghanistan.

Severe drought – probably due to climate change – had devastated the harvest for three years. The unstable – now that's an understatement – political situation had brought the shutters down on food distribution by relief agencies and the United Nations. Left with the no-win choice of stay and starve or go looking for food and starve, millions had chosen the latter.

Although extra motivation was unnecessary, fear of bombs of retribution or being forcibly recruited to fend off the 'invading hoards' had sped them on their way. Only to join others on the borders – and beyond – equally bereft of food, shelter and clean water. And it was to be winter in weeks – bringing bone-chilling temperatures of minus ten. Try that with skimpy blankets, meagre shelter and an empty belly.

Now, as I revise these words the focus has changed – to Southern Africa, where some fifteen million are at risk of starvation. Including children like seven-year-old

Manneranji from Malawi who is so frail she can barely stand. All this little girl, and thousands like her, has to eat are discarded corncobs – normally fed to chickens – ground into a sawdust type mixture to make a rancid-tasting 'porridge'.

For those like Manneranji across the great swathe of Southern Africa, the reasons for their plight are a complex mixture of the environment, incompetence and sheer despotism spread in unequal proportions depending on the country in question.

No doubt someone, somewhere, has glib answers as to why such inhuman treatment gets to be inflicted on genuinely innocent people with such regularity in world history. Like those who dare say that if only the poor worshipped the right God all would be well. If so, please keep them out of my arms' reach.

Meanwhile I find myself identifying with the many who escaped death by a whisker in New York on 11 September and similar though less spectacular tragedies since. Those who, even now, feel the aftershock of a massive wave of guilt. 'Why should "they" die while I survived?' is a surprising but very typical reaction in traumas like these. 'What right have I to live when they have been taken?'

Such emotions have a global counterpart in the light of what is being played out in Southern Africa and other parts of our grief-stricken world as I write. What did I do to deserve to be born in the privileged, affluent, ozone-destroying west? Where 'daily bread' is guaranteed in every sense of the word?

Indeed, in this context, the whingeing 'Why me, Lord?' so often heard when there's a small stone in our shoe of life takes on an entirely different meaning. And deserves an appropriate response.

21 But, isn't it mostly 'their fault'?

As a colleague of mine sat on the floor of a simple brick African home in southern Uganda he listened as seventeen-year-old Solomon confessed his greatest fear – that he would catch AIDS. And his younger brother Jude hung on every word.

It was easy to understand his fear. Solomon lives in Rakai, the region of Uganda notorious in the 1990s for the spiralling number of AIDS-related deaths. The boys' parents had both died from the disease several years ago – leaving Solomon, as the oldest child, to bring up his brother and three sisters.

Of course Africa is full of Solomons – young and old. In Africa, nearly one in ten already has the disease – in Zimbabwe and Botswana it is one in four. Few families remain unaffected in some way. Millions, like Solomon and Jude, become orphans, to be looked after by relatives or fend for themselves.

But isn't it all too easy to assume the ravaging impact of HIV/AIDS is partly if not mainly 'their fault'? That it is the result of widespread promiscuity? That if only they had 'morals like ours' they would not be in the mess they are in?

If there is even the hint of such a thought lurking at the back of your mind please think on. Yes, of course, not all sexual activity among Africans is within the framework of faithfulness in marriage, just as it isn't in the UK. However, the issue runs far deeper than that. Think of it this way . . .

Supposing in the UK, we had written off the first deaths as being the result of witchcraft, not disease. Because those deaths came mainly to businessmen in cities, and were assumed to be the result of the powerful magic of their business rivals, rather than something directly related to sexual behaviour. And supposing, as a result, the virus had become deeply ingrained in the 'system' before our government knew enough to respond. That's exactly what happened in Africa.

Supposing we had lacked both the money and the know-how to get the message out to the population – which was true of Africa. And when it came to doing so, our population was exactly like theirs – including many who were scattered, rural and illiterate.

Supposing we had had to face the prohibitive costs of screening blood supplies, a health system vastly more antiquated than our own, vast numbers of migrant workers separated from their families for long periods, the prevalence of rape by warring factions, and the impact of poverty, in leaving women with the often no-choice choice of either selling their bodies or seeing themselves and their children starve.

Supposing the basic cultural climate of the UK had been one where sex and its associated activities was something you just didn't talk about. And our government steadfastly refused to accept there was an issue to face, that there was a link between the HIV virus and death? Then what?

And though Africa's not exactly identical to the world's other HIV/AIDS hot spots, there are many similarities and parallels. Which means writing the global crisis off as all due to a lack of sexual morality is so far wide of the mark.

Come to that, just imagine how we would be faring given the circumstances of Africa and our own prevailing morality. What would our own death toll and head count of AIDS-generated orphans be like? How many Solomons would we have? Just think.

22 What price art in a hurting world?

Get ready to be screamingly angry. At least, I assume that will be your response.

It is possible you will remember the Taliban's destruction of the two ancient giant statues of Buddha that had been carved in a cliff face of golden sandstone. The Colossal Buddhas (as they are known) had gazed majestically across the fertile valley of Bamiyan for between 1,500 and 1,700 years.

It was one of the Taliban's last acts before the western troops invaded Afghanistan. Using mortar shells these happy hunters who included kite flying among their list of no-go activities went somewhat further by reducing these magnificent treasures to rubble in the name of religious orthodoxy.

But that's not what I am expecting you to get in a froth about, upsetting as it is. What I assume will raise your hackles even more is this. At a time when millions of Afghanis are still desperately poor and living in life threatening conditions there comes a new rage-maker.

There's a plan to spend up to £32 million to rebuild the Buddhas. Immoral or what?

But haven't we been there before? And is this really as scandalous as it at first seems?

In 1997 an earthquake in Italy left tens of thousands homeless – doing almost Taliban-sized damage to the magnificent painted ceiling of the Upper Basilica of St Francis of Assisi. And there were few screams of outrage when the ceiling was repaired at a cost of £12 million while in its shadows thousands were still living in squalor.

All of which leads me to two uncomfortable questions. First, is it only OK to recreate Christian art but not that of another culture?

Second, how does this all stack up with Jesus' acceptance of the seemingly wanton extravagance of a woman using almost priceless perfume on him? Perfume which, according to his accuser, should have been sold to help the poor – of which there were many.

[6]While Jesus was in Bethany in the home of a man known as Simon the Leper, [7]a woman came to him with an alabaster jar of very expensive perfume, which she poured on his head as he was reclining at the table.

[8]When the disciples saw this, they were indignant. 'Why this waste?' they asked. [9]'This perfume could have been sold at a high price and the money given to the poor.'

[10]Aware of this, Jesus said to them, 'Why are you bothering this woman? She has done a beautiful thing to me. [11]The poor you will always have with you, but you will not always have me.

(Matthew 26:6–11

Of course it's far less complicated to live in a black and white world of 'don't paint the walls until every last mouth has been fed'. But isn't it all more blurred at the edges than that? How else could I live with serving the poor from an office that is far from being utilitarianly basic? Or support projects, for example, where schools that are built include a budget for painting the walls and making things look nice?

And could it even be that in the economy of our oddly extravagant God, for some in Afghanistan the stability

that would come from seeing their ancient past rise again from the ashes may almost mean as much as a hot meal?
   Confusing isn't it?

Inequality

- Nearly half the world's population live on less than £1.40 per day.
- In the past 30 years, the gap between the world's richest twenty per cent and the poorest 20 per cent of people has tripled.
- The world's richest 225 people have a combined wealth equal to the annual income of almost half of the world's poorest people.
- The 48 least developed countries make up a mere 0.4 per cent of world trade.
- The developing world carries 90 per cent of the disease burden, yet benefits from only 10 per cent of the world's health resources.
- Europeans spend about £7.3 billion on ice cream each year – roughly what it would cost to provide safe water for every child on earth.
- The UK spends £199 million on eye make-up each year – which could provide 6 million children with vitamin A to prevent blindness.
- The UK spends £30 billion on golf each year – enough to provide basic healthcare, education and clean water to every human being on the planet.
- 20 per cent of the world's population live in countries that consume 86 per cent of the world's resources.
- It would take only 4 per cent of the wealth of the world's 225 richest people to provide the food, education and healthcare needed to end poverty.

23 Who would lend people like this £20m?

Would you lend your money to people so poor no reputable person will trust them with a bean? To people only qualified to stand in line for your money if they can't find anyone other than loan-sharks to cough up? People with no security to offer whatsoever and no guarantee they can ever pay you back?

Who in their right mind would do such a thing? Yet that's exactly what's happening in some of the world's poorest communities. I'm talking about one of the great under-told stories of development, the world of micro-enterprise. Here's something that's providing the means for a regular and reliable income and so transforming the lives of tens of thousands of people around the world.

Micro-enterprise is a tool that attacks the very roots of poverty. And its used by many agencies, including World Vision who currently have 'invested' over £20 million in some 175,000 people, confident they will use it to create a better future for themselves, their families and their communities.

The recipients of this seemingly naïve benevolence are not out to be mini Richard Bransons. Most simply want to put legs under an idea for a very small business, like selling flowers, making bricks, cutting hair or yielding more crops. For them it's about getting their hands on the equivalent of just a few pounds, based on submitting a simple business plan – and then being trusted to deliver it. Though there are others with their eyes on a much bigger world, like the woman's co-operative I saw in Bangkok. Their amazing silk flowers and needlework have already found markets in Scandinavia and Europe.

It is important to understand that what development agencies call micro-enterprise is far more sophisticated than just doshing out a few quid and hoping all goes well. What may sound like such a simple approach is anything but, when it's done right. And that's the way it has to be done if the change it is out to create is going to last.

The best micro-enterprise projects represent 'a helping hand with five fingers' according to Christopher Shore, the micro-enterprise director for the World Vision Partnership. These five fingers can be summed up as 1) *micro-finance* – the money needed to kick-start things; 2) *market access* – ways to sell the goods or services the money helps to create; 3) *appropriate technology* – the mechanical means to makes things work; 4) *information* – the knowledge that underpins everything; and 5) *know-how* – the training, job skills, education, and so on that holds it all together.

If that is already sounding somewhat dull and clinical, please allow me to walk you through the process – where you'll meet some of the amazing people involved on the way.

The 'first finger' on that helping hand is the issue of getting the money to the right people. Though some receive their loan as an individual, others are part of a group cross-guaranteeing each other. And for others still, the money goes to community savings groups of about twenty or so who then distribute it as loans to the members.

The uses such loans are put to are infinite. A family in Bangladesh used theirs to buy a boat rather than see a chunk of their catch sold to pay for a rented one. That simple move has lifted them above the poverty line. Others have bought sewing machines, rickshaws, and machines to make shoes out of old tyres. It is all down to what an aspiring entrepreneur can come up with.

Sometimes it is not just one loan that's involved but a series of them – with a new and often larger commitment made when the previous one is paid back. Typical is Ngare, a local barber in a Kenyan urban slum. With the aid of a loan he went hi-tech and bought electric hair clippers. He also renovated his small shop made out of corrugated sheeting. With that loan repaid, the next went on adding two extra chairs and putting linoleum on the floor – which also helped increase business.

A further loan meant Ngare could diversify. He bought a battery charger. With the domestic needs of most homes in the area powered by car batteries, he can now recharge up to seven batteries at a time. And when that loan is repaid his mind is set on purchasing a phone – so adding a further service to the community and further income for him and his family.

The second finger of micro-finance is the support needed to make sure the goods and services created get sold. Which means helping people identify and get to markets – local, regional, and even international. It is also about dealing with issues like fair trade and e-commerce.

Most examples of marketing and markets relate to their own neighbourhood. It can be as simple as loaning enough to buy a bicycle so a family can get their vegetables to market rather than sell them for a fraction of the income at the roadside. But at times there are some striking exceptions. People like Ruth, a single mum from a Kenyan shanty town, who has customers for her produce as far away as the US.

Financed through a micro-enterprise loan, Ruth is now selling flies to fishermen on the web. Every morning she spends two hours in one of the Internet cafés in Nairobi, surfing fishing sites for new patterns of flies and contacting her clients.

Ruth's idea came from meeting someone who knew how to tie flies but had no idea how to sell them. Three years later she already had four permanent staff, a supervisor and numerous outworkers for when demand gets hot.

But not all micro-enterprise initiatives are small stuff. Some involve sophisticated agriculture and marketing programmes, like the one serving poor farmers in northeastern Brazil. Here, World Vision Brazil organised farmers into a co-operative, assisted them in growing and packaging organic melons, and then marketed the crop to Brazilian and European supermarket chains under a fair trade logo. In only two years, the 500 family farmers in the co-operative saw their incomes nearly triple. And that's just the beginning.

Third, there's the technology that must often be addressed – everything from hand operated tools to things far more sophisticated. Under this heading also comes the introduction of new plant varieties and new animal breeds. Micro-enterprise includes helping people have the very best resources in order to make the most of their loan.

Fourth, there is the information that small local businesses need if they are to be managed efficiently and also flourish. Which means coming to terms with the world of the Internet, telephones, fax, databases, and so on. And that brings to mind my experience of being in a Ugandan town of some fifteen thousand or so people who were served by a telephone exchange of 224 phones – with only one line out to the wider world. That setting has to change if goods are to get sold more widely than at the local market.

It also brings to mind a story I heard of a village who, month by month, sold their crops to traders coming up the river who announced the going rate at which the villagers would have to sell. But then a development agency provided the village with a cell phone and thus the means to check the going rate themselves – with the result that they began to sell at a significantly higher price.

Fifth, there is the recognition that money, markets, technology and know-how are not enough to make the loans involved work their hardest. Good businesses, large and minute, can all benefit from training in job skills, and life skills – like delegation, managing time and others. And that's exactly what micro-enterprise programmes deliver.

Yet there is even more. Micro-finance also offers one much needed extra ingredient. One of its hallmarks is the way it releases a spirit of energy and creativity in its clients. They get excited about their future, energised about changing it, visionary about what could be the next step. Just because someone trusted them enough and held their hand every step of the way.

Of course, micro-enterprise development alone won't end poverty. It doesn't create safe water, schools, and healthcare or provide for other basic human needs that continue to go unmet by impoverished or indifferent governments. But, when micro-enterprise is integrated into an area development project, it can transform lives and offer much needed hope for the future. Which is what's happening out there.

But now let's go back to the issue of the loans – to those too poor to get them from anywhere else, and all the trust involved. Here's the big question. How much do you think comes back? Not much, the cynics would assume, in view of its impoverished recipients. In fact, it's about 97 per cent. Which shows you should never underestimate what can be done with courage, vision, trust, hard work – and £20 million.

24 They call it 'obligation'. You might call it 'genius'

When it comes to making a difference in the lives of the poor two phrases come fast to the frontal lobe – 'hand out' and 'hand up'. Let me add to this – 'obligation'. It describes a stunningly smart way to not only change the future for poor people but also to have them play a part themselves in changing things for others.

Here's the picture. You return as a refugee to your farm in Bosnia only to find your tractor has been severely trashed by the retreating forces. Tyres slashed, engine parts removed and the rest. There is no AA waiting to come to the rescue or Direct Line insurance to come tooting over the hill to kiss it all better. As a result there's no way you can work your farm and feed your family.

But now help arrives. Tractor experts from a relief and development agency – World Vision as it happens – go to work, repairing the damage and giving you back your future. And it hasn't cost you a diddly squit.

Once again you can plough your fields and scatter. But that's not the end of it. Here comes the 'obligation' bit.

Part of the deal was, with your tractor back in working order, you were to have an obligation. It was to someone else who also had a field to plough but no means to do so. And that is exactly what you do.

As a result, the 'hand out' which became a 'hand up' is multiplied in its impact. And there's more. In an ethnically divided community, the sharp brains behind the obligation concept have given you the field of someone from 'the other side'. So now you are also building a relationship – or 're-building' it more likely.

This is not an isolated concept. In the same community a small business that had its machinery re-commissioned is giving financial help for a year to those without work. A farmer helped get back on his feet is even giving milk to an elderly lady to feed her only companion – her cat.

It's a shrewd way to make aid go further and do more. On one hand there's 'hand out'. On the other 'hand up'. And to top it all 'obligation'. Dead clever these aid workers when you dig beneath the surface.

25 Girl talk – bad news and good

It is tough enough to be poor and a child. But even tougher if you are a girl – because you are likely to find the cards stacked against you at every turn. You are even less likely to ever see planet Earth as a girl. In some cultures, you may be selectively aborted. In others you'll be killed or abandoned at birth. And it's not much better from there on in.

Research shows if you're a girl in a poor community you'll get less food, healthcare and education than your brothers. You'll work longer hours than boys, receive less training and less pay. You'll be treated as a second-class citizen socially, legally and economically.

As a girl you are more likely to be sexually exploited by men you know or by foreigners engaged in child prostitution and pornography. Being seen as an economic and social burden means you are likely to be married off early – becoming a bride and even a mother while you are still a child. And if you live in the wrong country – and there are at least twenty-five 'wrong countries' – you face mutilation to your genitals to guarantee your virginity.

All this – and more – adds up to the reality that life for millions of the world's female children is dismal. Some experts even claim conditions for girls in many countries are worse than at any time in history.

Yet the World Bank states that investment in girls, particularly through education, is one of the most effective investments a country can make in its journey out of poverty. They say *'When a country educates its girls, it raises economic productivity, lowers maternal and infant mortality, reduces fertility rates, improves the health, well-being and educational prospects of the next generation, promotes sounder management of environmental resources, and reduces poverty.'*

Big words. But is anyone doing anything about them? The good news is some fifty governments have 'seen it' and developed National Plans of Action that face up to the needs and rights of girls. And many development agencies – including World Vision – are highly active on the issue too, creating policies and strategies focused on the needs and future of girl children: designing development programmes that offer equal opportunities. Supporting the leadership development of girls. And much more.

And not before time.

Guatemala – Girls for peace and justice

- *For an exceptional example of giving girls priority, look no further than Guatemala's The Ninas de Shalom (Young Women of Peace and Justice) Programme.*

- *In the national culture, Guatemalan girls often marry between the ages of thirteen and fifteen with no choice of husband. Many start having children right after marriage. But the Shalom Programme gives them an alternative by teaching them about their own rights and how to run their own businesses.*

- *Girls attend two-year training courses. The centre includes an organic demonstration farm which helps the girls learn about nutrition and earning money through raising small animals and growing vegetables and flowers.*

- *The tutors provide ongoing support when the girls return home; the girls then organise clubs where they teach up to 10 more girls what they have learned.*

26 Spreading like wildfire – a positive experience

HIV/AIDS is spreading around the globe like wildfire – and now I too am a 'victim'. So if you've ever wondered what it feels like to be HIV positive – not physically but emotionally and psychologically – I have a smidgen of the answer.

I can tell you because I 'caught' the virus recently – as did a bunch of others when we took part of an amazing simulation experience. And even as a 'virtual HIV positive' the raw emotions it triggered for me and others were eye-opening.

Picture thirty people in a room with a skilled facilitator. In a circle facing inward one of the number gets a secret tap on their shoulder and so becomes the one single 'HIV positive' person in the group. At a signal we follow the instructions we have been given and begin randomly shaking hands – allowed to shake as few or as many as we like but under orders to press the flesh at least once.

However, that one 'positive' member must scratch the palm of each of the hands they shake – the secret sign indicates contact with 'the virus'. Those receiving the sign must, in turn, pass on the same signal as they shake hands and so on. Following which comes the moment of reckoning.

All this flesh pumping only took a few minutes, if that. Some had been shy about it all, doing little more than shake the one obligatory hand. Just a few had been much more gregarious and promiscuous. And now an alarmingly large group drawn from the total participants, including me, sit in a circle holding envelopes. We are those who have received the sign at least once, indicating that, somewhere down the line, the history of our handshake experience had been tainted. We have been exposed to the risk of becoming HIV positive.

In our envelopes are the results of our 'test'. Figuratively speaking we'd had unprotected sex with someone who had unprotected sex with someone who . . . Now what? Would I get away with it? Or would the risk I had taken become an internal time bomb?

The emotions are running. I had shaken only two hands but was I to pay the price for their sexual history? And in poor communities there are countless other ways to become HIV positive than through sexual activity – from contaminated blood to un-sterilised scalpels to nursing mothers passing on the virus. In every case, putting others at risk.

Watched by those who had survived the exercise unscathed we opened the envelopes. Those with 'no' sighed a simulated gasp of relief, confessing afterwards that strange as it may sound their reaction was not as simulated as might be imagined. They traced, deep down, a sense of relief that was but a minute sample of what someone genuinely in this situation would feel.

And those with 'yes' – like me – later confessed to the sense of fear, hopelessness, doom and lack of hope that hit them from somewhere deep within. For fleeting moments we became part of the family of the 5 million new people a year for whom becoming infected by the virus becomes the real thing.

The exercise, called Wildfire, was developed by the United Nations. It aims to help people move beyond the staggering statistics, to gain an insight into how it might feel to be at risk of HIV/AIDS infection, to be tested, and to get a result. And so to be of far more value to those for whom the experience is anything other than an afternoon's charade.

It works.

For more information on Wildfire go to
http://www.undp.org/hiv/publications/toolkit/sample10.html.

27 Holding hands in the dark

When it comes to prayer, why do we always feel there have to be words to say? And exactly the right words?

Confronted with the most appalling tragedies – be it decimated twin towers, sexually abused children, mass genocide or whatever – our reflex reaction is to become responsible for telling God exactly what he should do next. To go looking for nice rounded prayers of the 'ask, seek, knock' kind Jesus spoke of in Matthew 7.

Already beset with circumstances way beyond our ability to comprehend, we drive our feeble minds to now deliver the Almighty's action plan. Anything less, we feel, is not 'prayer'. I know that's what happens because I've been there. Like that recurring dream of being caught in a grocery store wearing nothing but a T-shirt – feeling exposed and guilty for having so little to say.

But is that really what God expects of us when faced with the incomprehensible? To launch into the articulate when reeling breathless – like a boxer staggering from a low blow?

It has taken me far too long to realise that the answer is a gloriously resounding 'no'.

In circumstances like these – and many others where we are overwhelmed – God gives us permission just to gasp in his presence. To soak up the pain and present it to him. Indeed, this is what it means to be an intercessor – a 'go-between' – one who stands between what 'is' and the God who knows exactly how it 'ought to be'.

At times words are bound to fail us because we fall somewhat short of being the all-knowing and all-powerful God. We are simply those who also feel the pain of his broken world and want to bring it to him. So together we – he and us – can hold hands in the dark. To know he is there – whether we feel it or not. To know he cares desperately and passionately – whether there is evidence or not.

And to trust his promise that his Spirit will take the unspoken utterings of our inner being and make sense of them to his own ears. Because, as Paul reminded the Christians in Rome, 'We do not know what we ought to pray for but the Spirit himself intercedes for us with groans that words cannot express' (Romans 8:26).

28 When seeing really is believing

The place, a rural – and I do mean 'rural' – village in Cambodia. With drought for half the year and floods for the other. Where to be hungry is normal, education is sparse and life fragile, particularly for those under five.

The setting – a 'deck' open to the elements but for its wooden roof, and set on stilts ready for the rains that will eventually come. The audience – me, with about sixty sponsored children at my feet looking on. The occasion – the members of the Village Development Committee presenting me with a report of their gradual emergence from poverty. And it was here seeing truly became believing.

In my head was all the theory about changing the future of poor communities. That creating lasting development – the jargon is 'sustainable' – has to involve giving genuine ownership to those whose lives are to be transformed. That *they* are those who must do the work – evaluating *their* own need, setting *their* own priorities and being the real change-makers. This was the theory and now it was coming to life before my own eyes.

With the help of huge sheets of paper I received an amazing conducted tour of what is, what needs to be and what this most needy group of people are doing to bridge the gap. It was all their own work, thanks to the highly skilled input of a specialist Community Development Worker and their team.

With the help of a range of PLAs – that's Participatory Learning Activities to the uninitiated - they'd been given the help to create a map showing the 'streets' and 'landmarks' of the patch they called 'home'. With the same kind of help they had also drawn up an inventory of what they had – the people, ranked by age and level of poverty; the houses, even including what they were made of; the animals, all counted down to the last chicken; and much more.

And with more of the same help they'd also created an amazing and highly sophisticated assessment of their village's needs. They talked me through the contents of a large flipchart, and animatedly explained what the real issues were and why. Which impacted the other. Where they had needed to act first.

Next they itemised the help they'd been given to change their future – things they had no way of providing themselves. The quantity of high-grade rice seed down to the last kilo. The number of chickens, pigs and other livestock received on loan – to be repaid when the breeding season was over. The number of wells and pumps provided. And so on and so on and so on.

Here were people who, probably only two or three years earlier, had been bowed down by their circumstances with no road map for the future. Now I was looking at a group of barely educated and somewhat unsophisticated people who had it more together than many small businesses in the west. They had a vision, a plan, a budget – and were getting the skills training and additional resources to make lasting change a reality.

Before my eyes was a group for whom life had once been hopeless beyond words. Yet now I could see that they were facing their future with confidence. I'd seen the theory put into practice – but I'd seen even more. Because now, forever etched in my mind, is the vision of the proud and positive faces of the committee and the wide eyes of the sponsored children.

Seeing is believing and I can only ask 'One day, won't all development look like this?' I'd like to believe it will.

Clean and safe water

- 1.3 billion people have no access to clean water.
- In the developing world contaminated water accounts for 80 per cent of all disease.
- Contaminated water claims the lives of five million children a year.
- Every day 1.3 billion people lack the 25 litres of water needed for drinking, sanitation and food preparation in order to survive; while the average UK citizen uses 150 – 200 litres for things like showering, bathing, laundry, drinking, cooking, cleaning, gardening and car washing.

29 Counted as equal? Or not counted at all?

Amid the spectacular pageantry of the opening ceremony of the 2002 Commonwealth Games two images captured me. One, of a young adult with Down's Syndrome. The other, a young girl in a wheelchair.

But these were not passive spectators in the crowd, objects of pity, destined to only watch from the stands while much envied able-bodied and able-minded athletes, dancers and 'others' celebrated. In fact, exactly the opposite.

These two were at the very heart of the high-energy celebrations. They were out in the centre of the arena, as part of the exuberant throng. Equal participants, on equal terms. A heart-moving, eye-moistening sight to behold.

And a sound to behold was the Games' International President underlining that these games would be different, because disabled athletes were here on an equal basis. No separate tally of medals for them. Their achievements were to be counted as of equal worth to those of everyone else in their national team.

It marked a significant and groundbreaking change of attitude, and it has something to say to those of us concerned about the poor worldwide. Because some estimate as many as one in five of those living in poor communities are disabled.

And though our own attitudes in the west have changed, this is far from a universal experience. A child with a disability is more often seen as an embarrassment to the family, a punishment from God or a burden too heavy to bear. No 'equal terms' for them with supportive government legislation about equal access and equal rights. Instead they are an object of shame, prejudice, superstition or apathy – paying a high price as a result.

As a far too often result, those who are most in need are hidden from the public eye – by their families or in separate institutions. They become shut out from all that's available to fully able children – including education, social interaction, employment and the dignity of helping their community make a journey out of poverty.

Disability in numbers

Behind every one of these statistics is a person

- *There are an estimated 600 million people with disabilities across the globe – one in ten of the world population. Of these, an estimated 120-150 million are children.*
- *World Vision estimates up to one in five of people living in poor communities are disabled.*
- *Research shows violence and abuse are three times more likely to happen to a disabled child.*
- *In Nepal, where marriage is the norm for women, four out of five women with disabilities are reported to be unmarried.*
- *In China, more than half of disabled women over eighteen years old are unmarried.*

Not untypical is Cho Cho Myaing, who has never left the Burmese (Myanmar) village home where she was born more than thirty years ago. Physically unable to move around, who knows what she could have achieved given the opportunities? Education, marriage, work and the ability to support herself and her family? Instead Myaing has nothing but an uncertain future, while the mother she depends on grows more frail by the day.

For those working with the poor, a hungry child – belly bloated from malnutrition – is hard to miss. But it takes time, commitment and tenacity to identify this hidden face of poverty and to tackle it, including the attitudes at its root.

Yet doing so will mean the difference between life and death, between hope for the future or despair at the years ahead for some of God's most fragile creatures.

30 Something fishy about development

You know about the 'teach a man to fish' stuff. And how it makes sense. That it's better to put knowledge in people's hands rather than hand outs that will eventually run out. But do you know how deep this concept runs in the world of development – even down to having a jargon all of its own?

The jargon – clumsy and, at times, confusing – is a helpful way to understand how 'fishy' work with poor communities ought to be. Its key phrase is 'capacity building'. Which has nothing to do with how much something contains. Or with bricks and mortar. It's about the capacity of a person, organisation or society to make a difference to their future.

For example, to stick with the fish illustration, the more skills you give a hungry man the greater 'capacity' he has to feed himself – and others too. And if you give him the skills to teach others to fish, the greater 'capacity' the village has to change their future.

The teaching that takes place 'builds capacity'. Activities like this, which increase people's ability to shape their future, are going on all over the place – where development agencies are doing it right.

It's not just about individuals. The main emphasis of the capacity-building activities of development agencies is on groups and the local community as a whole. Identifying and bringing together the leaders of a village to create their own action plan builds their capacity. Providing training in planning and management builds their capacity.

Showing them how to make a case for grants from their municipality – and giving them the self-esteem to apply for them – builds their capacity. Bringing reconciliation to communities committed to knocking lumps off each other builds their capacity. The examples are endless.

Of course, those paid to do this kind of thing have a way to make it sound more complex – and to them it probably is. They throw in phrases like 'social intervention' and explain that it all grew out of 'a realisation that more was needed than technical intervention and economic solutions'.

Whatever, the thing is, it matters big time – for two obvious reasons. First, capacity building (it hurts to write jargon but sometimes you have to) is more likely to bring lasting change. Second, this kind of action puts the emphasis on the poor themselves being their own solutions. It is people based – putting the poor where they ought to be, at the very centre of the process.

When thinking about changing the future of the poor the easy bit for us to understand is what we can see. Things like wells for safe water, clinics for healthcare and schools for education. But look a little deeper and we

also ought to be seeing something going on that's very
fishy indeed.

31 The ABC of HIV/AIDS and low-flying pigs

In this age of recreational sex, where the only perversion is not doing it, something amazing has happened at the United Nations. In the fight against the incoming tidal wave of HIV/AIDS they are now calling for morality and spiritual beliefs to be at the forefront of the campaign. Not condoms for everyone. But something very different.

They are now adding their substantial weight to that of the many whose message on how to avoid the virus and its horrific consequence is simply ABC. That's – Abstinence, Being faithful to one partner and Consistently using a condom. Or to put it more fully – Don't do it now. When you do, don't ever do it with anyone else. And whatever you do, always use a condom.

This so un-PC approach is aimed at the young and highlighted in an excellent UN report designed to help reverse the spread of HIV among young people. Instead of the expected and too often heard 'do what you want but be careful' message here is a breath of fresh air – and much needed reality.

The report highlights the young as the age group most vulnerable to infection. Our planet is already home for almost twelve million fifteen to twenty-four year olds infected by HIV's ticking time bomb of death – with 6,000 new cases added daily. And please don't blame them.

Too many live in countries with a conspiracy of silence – denying them the information that could save their lives – or lack the mass media to get the word out. As a result, in large numbers of poor countries, over three-quarters remain ignorant of the three main ways to protect themselves.

The solution, says the UN welcomingly, is to make the young the priority, to fight their ignorance and encourage responsible lifestyles. But there is more than ABC in this report.

Tucked among the recommendations for helping young people steer clear of dangerous sexual encounters – things like having good relationships with parents and teachers, feeling valued, and having a sense of hope and exposure to positive values – is the value of having spiritual beliefs. That's right, abstinence and spiritual values being promoted by the good old UN. Look out for low-flying pigs.

Look out too for smiles on the faces of Christian agencies like World Vision – who have been responding to the HIV/AIDS agenda with exactly these priorities. They had it right all along.

This 'Young People and HIV/AIDS' report can be reached via_www.unaids.org.

32 Time to tell the truth about Child Sponsorship

Let's face it, Child Sponsorship is nothing more than a cynically manipulative way to wring money out of people. Right? It's all about exploiting vulnerable children, putting a burden on an already struggling community and adding to the charity's overhead costs. Right?

If so, agencies using Child Sponsorship to fund their work with the poor need to think again. Fast.

Recently I came face to face – to be more accurate face to knee cap – with sixty or so sponsored children in a World Vision project. The experience made the accusations even more pertinent. Were these bright eyed and remarkably un-fidgety kids really no more than charity fodder? And the rest of their community reluctant participants in the whole charade?

The children had sat attentively listening to the report I had been given by their Village Development Committee. Together we had heard the reasons why their community were poor, what needed to happen, what the villagers were doing about it and the help they were getting from outside.

As a visiting 'interested party' – and an honoured guest – I was invited to say a few words. I made the children my focus. 'How many of you are sponsored children?' I asked. I could almost smell their pride, as every hand was raised, backs straightened and faces beamed.

'And how many of you write letters to your sponsors?' Their pride went into overdrive – and the penny dropped. These kids were absolutely thrilled to be playing their own role in seeing their community move out of poverty. They had listened so well because this was their story too and they were proud to be genuine participators.

Over the next few days I watched local World Vision staff diligently photographing and documenting new children that the community had themselves identified to be sponsored. I saw the village people gaining life-enhancing skills through managing the paperwork that sponsorship necessitates in order to keep responsible records and manage the relationship with support offices. I saw the changes that had come from the sponsorship income being used to benefit the whole community.

Meanwhile, in the UK and all round the world, those who had taken the step to become child sponsors were experiencing a unique relationship with a community that was moving towards standing on its own feet. They too were active participants in the development process and being greatly enriched by the experience.

In fact when World Vision UK spent time at a senior leadership level at looking to the future, the whole issue of Child Sponsorship was put on the table with the conclusion that even if there were other ways to fund the work of development they would still go for Child Sponsorship. Because of the impact it has on the children and the sponsors themselves. No one could think of a better way – or one that even came close – to enrich the lives of everyone concerned.

Of course, not every agency does Child Sponsorship in exactly the same way. But most of the major agencies involved have worked together to create a charter for good behaviour and best practice. To be specific, ActionAid, Christian Children's Fund of Great Britain, International Care and Relief, Plan International UK and World Vision UK – who hold each other accountable for clear communication to supporters and responsible actions in the sponsorship programmes.

This includes a commitment to being sure sponsors know how their support is being used. In World Vision's case, this means taking care to stress that the money doesn't go directly to the child or their family. And for very good reasons. Not least because of the issue of favouritism in and between families. And, even more so, because doing so significantly reduces an agency's ability to work with the very poorest in communities.

If the plan is to give money to a family to support their child's education then you can only do so where a school already exists. Give money direct to a family for their child's healthcare and there has to be a clinic already in the community. And so on.

But pool the resources, all the time giving special attention to the exceptionally poor children the village has identified for sponsorship, and you can work with the poorest of the poor. Those pooled contributions can become a means for all the children and the whole community to eventually have the basic essentials for life.

Does Child Sponsorship ever go wrong? Of course. Is that a good enough reason to abandon the concept? Not in my eyes. After all, when you make a long-term financial promise to a poor community you'd better know how you are going to keep it. And when you can do so in a way that enriches the lives of the children, the adults and the donors alike, that's more than good enough for me.

33 It's the Frankenstein Factor

As I write, vast supplies of grain that would go a very long way to meeting the needs of Africa's hungry are languishing in storage. But as people starve the food just sits there. Meanwhile, India has rejected a large shipment of desperately needed food aid in the form of maize and soya, intended for areas suffering from chronic malnutrition.

Why? Because in both instances – and in not a few others like it – the offered food is genetically modified maize: GM. Or, as it has been dubbed by its opponents, 'Frankenstein Food'. And many governments and aid agencies believe GM grain may well be bad news in the long term.

The pro-GM argument goes 'People are desperately hungry. This food is good enough for millions of Americans. Stop being pedantic and let's get it to the hungry – fast.'

The other voice says, 'The quick answer could prove to be a long-term disaster. Even if GM grain is safe to eat – and there are still major concerns – this is not the only issue. What if it is planted? Who knows what the long-term impact on the grain crop of the nations involved might turn out to be? More than that, GM corn needs expensive fertiliser. And where's that produced and sold? In the affluent and wonderfully benevolent west. So such a generous gift could have a very pricey payback in the long run.'

Responsible aid and development agencies are committed to a long-term view and to doing what is genuinely in the best interests of those who are poor. That's one reason they place such emphasis on environment-friendly farming methods. These are not only healthy but protect the poor from the commercial interests of those with fertiliser to sell.

But what a cleft stick to be in! As an agency, facing widespread famine and impending death on a massive scale, do you sell out the future of the poor for the sake of their short-term survival? Do you dump your convictions in order to feed hungry mouths at the expense of the future well-being of the community?

Do you overlook the fact that the poor are to be denied the dignity and right to have a say over what they eat in the way that does not happen in the developed world? That they are to be offered no choice other than to accept the judgement of the west that GM is safe to eat?

The alternative is desperately to seek other solutions – which is what aid agencies have been doing and why tons of GM maize still languishes in storage. Those 'other solutions' include finding alternative sources of emergency food aid. And arguing for the simplest solution of all – that the maize could be milled before it is delivered, thus making it edible but not plantable.

Such a simple solution would end the standoff and bring desperately needed food to thousands of malnourished and vulnerable people. So why isn't it happening?

34 Every picture tells a story

Pictures of children with swollen bellies, spindly legs and fly-blown faces. That's the way to lever money from an indifferent public on behalf of the poor. Isn't it?

But what about the poor themselves? How do they feel about being seen as no more than helpless objects of pity? What does such a blatant invasion of their dignity – as those created in the image of God – do to them? And to us?

Questions like these have driven responsible aid agencies to think deeply about the way they portray the poor. For example, the Disasters Emergency Committee, which co-ordinates major disaster appeals, insists '*In our information, publicity and advertising we shall recognise disaster victims as dignified humans, not hopeless objects.*' The Red Cross similarly promises to recognise disaster victims as '*dignified human beings, not objects of pity*'.

Representatives from aid and development agencies in the European Union met in 1980 and committed to '*Avoiding catastrophic or idyllic images which appeal to charity and lead to a clear conscience rather than a consideration of the root problems.*'

World Vision is one agency to have gone further. As a result there's an absolute commitment to avoid '*apocalyptic or pathetic images, or idyllic or exotic images, or generalisations which do not accurately reflect the nature of the situation*'. Out too are '*images which foster a sense of northern superiority or portray the people we work with as dependent, poor and powerless*'.

More than that, particular care is taken with images of women who '*are often portrayed as dependent victims or simply do not figure in the picture*'. And children are protected by making sure they are '*adequately clothed*' and never in '*poses that could be interpreted as sexually suggestive.*'

Of course, the way the poor are conveyed is about more than pictures. As the European agencies agreed in 1989, '*People's ability to take responsibility for themselves must be highlighted; The causes of poverty (political, structural or natural) should be apparent . . . to enable the public to become aware of the history and real situation.*'

And all this is not just about saying 'no' to exploiting the poor. It's also about not exploiting the donor. They too are made in God's image. They too must be treated with dignity. Images that exploit the poor exploit them also.

As World Vision's operating principles state, '*we shall not exploit, nor manipulate, the heart of the donor for the sake of the poor. Nor shall we exploit the poor for the sake of meeting the needs of the donor. Our commitment is to both*'. And you may be surprised how many other agencies feel and act in exactly the same way.

Don't you think such a commitment is worth smiling about? Then please face this way and say 'cheese'.

35 Without a leg to stand on

Every twenty minutes, someone in the world is injured or killed by a landmine, or UXO (unexploded ordnance), usually civilians and often children. Which is hardly surprising seeing there is so much of this stuff lurking out there.

To drink in the size of the problem, ponder on the fact that an estimated 300,000 intact bombs litter Vietnam's soil. Yemen has as many as one million landmines left behind by three civil wars since 1962. Angola has about eight million landmines strewn across its blood-soaked land due to successive conflicts over the past forty years. Which is just for starters.

And they are doing more than kill and maim. This cocktail of landmines and other unexploded leftovers from war makes fields un-ploughable, homes un-liveable, puts additional pressure on the overstretched medical resources of poor nations, and diverts the efforts of the aid agencies from doing something more worthwhile.

The culprits are charming items of human ingenuity. Like the innocently named 'Bomblets'. And cluster bombs – *designed* to detonate on impact but having the same level of efficiency as most other 'public service' industries, leaving them permanently waiting for the unwary.

All this has an impact. For example, more than ninety landmine accidents have been reported throughout Angola over the first six months of this year. Most occurred on roads, farms, game areas and near sources of water. Globally the number injured from landmines and unexploded ordnances runs to 20,000 each year.

It is hardly surprising seeing that 110 million landmines lie in the ground on every continent. And most minefields are unmarked as the result of their warning signs having either disintegrated or been used for firewood.

What's being done? In Angola for example there's a programme to train primary school teachers who will then reach children through their classes who will in turn pass on the awareness to their families and communities. And get the message to children who don't go to school through drama, songs and talks at public places such the streets and health clinics.

Landmine landmarks

- *Over 300,000 children have already been disabled by landmines.*
- *Mines can cost as little as £2 to manufacture but over £600 to clear.*
- *False arms or legs for landmine victims cost on average almost £2,000 each.*

It is urgent because of the dangers that wait. And with famine abroad in parts of Africa it will get worse. Those scavenging for food will look further and further afield and be increasingly at risk.

An enemy too is simple human foolishness. Like the death of an old man in Laos – a contender for the Darwin Awards were it not so tragic. Investigators found a crowbar, wooden mallets and various pieces of unexploded bomb at the scene. The man had been trying to break down bomblets to use the explosives for fishing.

If that sounds foolish, try this. The US military are now working on 'intelligent mines' – that throw themselves across minefields to confuse and confound an enemy. When a breach occurs, the mines will respond by hopping automatically into new positions.

This great creation is to be called the 'Self-Healing Minefield'. It ought to be off limits until people and communities have the same self-healing ability.

For details of the Campaign Against Landmines go to http://www.icbl.org.

For what's being done to help landmine victims go to http://www.landminesurvivors.org.

36 There's always a way

When a government says 'no' to anyone helping the churches or sharing the good news about Jesus, what can a Christian agency, committed to seeing God's kingdom grow, do?

That's an issue agencies like World Vision face every day, due to the diverse situations in which they work. And, faced with an official brick wall, there have been some highly creative ways round it.

It matters because such Christian agencies see spiritual renewal as an essential ingredient in the process involved in seeing the quality of life improve for poor communities. If people can come to understand why they exist and what they have been called to do they will behave very differently. And, at the same time, strong churches have a key role to play in the lives of poor people. Indeed, they should be the very best news the poor can have.

So what can be done when a restrictive government forbids church leaders from holding a Pastors Conference designed to enrich their lives and strengthen their churches? The answer is to look for what can be done – and in this case there was no ban on holiday coach tours.

So World Vision provided the funds for church leaders to book a tour of the country. Not having been able to meet together for over twenty years, you can imagine how much they had to share and to learn.

For ten life-enriching days these pressured pastors worshipped, prayed, watched videos and deepened their relationships. And the sights of interest that they visited? Other pastors!

At a time when it is all too easy to do nothing because 'nothing can be done' thank God for, and be inspired by, the courage and ingenuity of others. And let's take up the challenge to think outside the box more often ourselves.

37 Sometimes answers really do grow on trees

I never discovered his name. But, if this member of one of the world's poorest communities had a nickname it must have been 'Mr Excited'. His enthusiasm oozed. And its focus was the rough and ready drawing of a tree held in his fervent hands.

The tree was adorned with an intriguing assortment of words, written over the roots and branches. For Mr Excited this was a road map to a better future, for him and his whole village. Let me explain.

When a development specialist enters a poor community they know most of what needs to be done. Which makes it tempting to simply deliver a blast of 'this is the way it is' and 'this is what you need to do.'

But the best development practitioners know better: that people learn far more from discovery than from being told. That it is as people encounter issues and investigate the implications that lights go on and they become active players in the process of change.

That's why good development practice involves the poor in learning through their own discovery and analysis: – an approach known as Participatory Learning. Facilitators make it possible for the group themselves to identify the issues and the best solutions. Not those beyond their knowledge – like the best kind of wells to dig or crops to plant. But on their community's fundamental needs, why things are the way they are, the impact it is all having and the best next steps to take.

Which brings us back to Mr Excited and his tree. The tree and the words on it were the result of some hard participatory learning by village representatives.

Forget the 'we'll talk and you'll listen' approach

Helping communities identify their own solutions to their needs and problems is not rocket science. As these examples used in development show.

Problem-solving

On a large piece of paper, draw a table with four columns. In the first column get the participants to list the main problems they face. In the second column to list the possible solutions to each of the problems. In the third, what prevents them from solving the problem. And in the fourth, what will help them solve the problem.

Socio-economic dimensions

A way to identify households in greatest need is to make cards or slips of paper, each with one household name written on it. Then ask villagers or participants to sort the cards into piles according to what they perceive as their wealth.

Ranking their needs

Helping a village understand and 'own' what needs to be done first is an exercise for a grid on a large piece of paper. In the left hand column they write the issues they face – no safe water, little food, no education, lack of healthcare, etc. Then each can distribute their three stones to what they regard as the most urgent need – either all in one go or spread in any way they wish.

Time line

On a horizontal line, ask people to mark major events in the community, with the rough dates. Talk with them how changes have taken place.

Having identified the things that kept them poor they assigned each to a different Problem Tree. And on this one – emblazoned across the trunk – were the words 'Lack of Food'.

On the branches were added the things that 'grow' on such a 'lack of food' tree. One branch traced how lack of food led to poor health, which led to sickness and death. Another that lack of food led to children having to scavenge for it, which led to them not going to school, which led to them having little chance of jobs in the future. And so on.

This simple exercise had taken the village's focus from the problem to the consequences. Now they could see the big picture. But there were also the roots, on which were the reasons for the problem. 'Why lack of food?' Mr Enthusiastic read out loud from the drawing – eyes blazing with understanding. 'Because only one crop each year.'

'Why lack of food?' he continued. 'Because no good irrigation system. Why lack of food? Because no store to save extra rice. Why no food? Because . . .' Now eyes were on the solutions and what could be done. And not just for this one problem but also for all the major issues contributing to their poverty.

What a journey this village had been through. In their hands were the results of their own analysis; now they felt ownership, knew what had to happen next, what they could do themselves and what outside aid was essential.

No wonder Mr Excited was excited! As are the thousands like him now finding their way out of poverty because of those wise enough to help them ask the right questions.

Food and hunger

- 840 million people are underfed.
- Food production must be doubled by 2020 if there is to be enough to feed the world's population.
- In developing countries four out of every ten children are stunted through malnutrition.

38 Written on the palms of their hands

It began with a request for an autograph and ended in glorified chaos. With a major lesson about our relationship with God at the heart of it.

Surrounding me was a myriad of flashing Thai smiles – courtesy of the junior school pupils at Pianpin Anusorn School, Bangkok. I was there to see their remarkable Luncheon Club. It had been created to make sure the 700 children – mostly World Vision sponsored children from Bangkok slums – had one good meal a day.

The most obvious answer would have been to raise the money and ship in a meal a day courtesy of western benefactors. World Vision Thailand had a sharper idea. One now spreading across many parts of Asia.

With adult help the children are growing their own vegetables and rearing fish, frogs and chickens. It's part of a far-ranging and impressive Area Development Programme that's gradually transforming a whole community.

The arrival of this foreigner was a huge event. I'd watched them line up with their metal plates for their nutritious meal, all giggles and smiles as the result of the invasion of their space. Now, with lunch over, a crowd gathered on the school steps to smile and wave – with lots more junior school giggling. It was then the request for the autograph came. And then another and another.

Inspiration was needed to make this a more productive exercise. Taking a little hand I drew on its palm a simple face – eyes, nose, and a mouth. Gasps of joy were matched by a forest of equally small hands, each eagerly requesting a face of their own.

Now in my stride I made sure every single face was different. Curly hair here. A long tongue there. Teeth or none. A grin or a frown. Even freckles – though on reflection I am not sure Thai faces ever have them. But it was all the best way I could think to convey to each of these children that they were unique and special – to God and to me.

Just as they probably didn't understand the freckles they probably didn't grasp the message either. And, even if they did, they may have forgotten it quickly – because black felt tip washes off.

For my part I hope the memory takes a long time to fade. Because in my world of development, where you are determined to change the way things will be for as many as you can, it is all too easy to think numbers and not people.

If Jesus had our name 'engraved on the palms of his hands' can't we at least try to see people as individuals too?

39 Is the church big enough for the world?

Two questions. The first I am sure you'll see as a no-brainer, the second as somewhat strange. Together they may challenge one of your most fundamental assumptions about the church being good news to the poor.

First the no-brainer. 'Is God big enough for the church?' Such a dumb inquiry hardly seems worth the breath or the brainpower involved voicing it. Or in voicing the answer 'yes'. But now for the second question. 'Is the church big enough for the world?' Or, to flesh it out a bit, 'Is the church big enough to achieve all God wants done in his world?'

For many of us, our reflex response is a 'yes' – every bit as resounding as our first reply. In fact we somehow feel that if God is big enough for us then it's our responsibility to behave as though, with his help, we are big enough for the needs of the world. And that the real problem is we are not good enough at doing what we should be doing.

Of course, those outside the church – or nominal participants – would wonder what the above two paragraphs are about anyway. To them these words would seem to come from another planet. All this talk about God and the church being 'big enough'. But those on the inside have a very different perspective – particularly regarding what the church is expected to do in God's world.

And if some of that has rubbed off on you – and you imagine God's plan is for the church to do it all – please put some realism to work. Take a moment to think about the vast scale of need in our world, where a child dies of poverty every three seconds and a billion lack access to safe, disease free drinking water.

Is all this something God expects only the church to shoulder? Is it really his intention that great swathes of the globe are to be consigned to a wrenched and hopeless future until the church where they are is strong enough to respond and has the vision and resources to do so? Until its members worldwide have enough of their own money – and the generosity to match – to finance the solutions? And have all the expertise and person-power available to do the job?

Is it really all down to the church?

Let's get real. Is all this meant to fall on the shoulders of the church alone?

- *1.2 billion people on our planet live in absolute poverty.*
- *Every 3.6 seconds someone dies due to hunger and malnutrition.*
- *Nearly ten million children a year die before their first birthday and twelve million before their fifth – mainly due to hunger and malnutrition.*
- *More than a billion people lack access to safe drinking water.*
- *Around 850 million of the world's adults are illiterate and two-thirds are women.*
- *Worldwide there are twelve million refugees and 25 million displaced in their own country.*

But if not, why do those in the church at times act as though this is so? How does the church do this? By so often behaving as if 'God's best' is for us to raise money exclusively from Christians and use it to work exclusively in partnership with those churches or other Christian agencies who are part of a poor community. And that anything else is somewhat 'tainted' and not authentically Christian. A grey second best and a mucky compromise.

I am not knocking such endeavours because they have a vital role to play in the total picture. But the subconscious attitudes that can so easily lurk behind such an exclusive approach are dangerous. And such a method will never be enough, on its own, to bring about the global justice that's on God's heart.

Which means there is a challenge for the churches to think and act differently. To celebrate every move for justice whether it comes from us or not. To pray 'your kingdom come' expecting God to answer through more than just the work and initiatives of the world church.

It means churches and Christian agencies finding ways to harness the goodwill, finances, and commitment of those who don't share their beliefs. It means Christian agencies engaging in partnerships with communities where the church is not yet flourishing – recognising it is genuinely Christian to tough it out in nations and communities where they may be almost all of the body of Christ that's there.

It will also mean being brave in ways the church is not very good at. Let me try this one on you. One of the very best and most effective agencies in addressing HIV/AIDS around the globe – and that is something of an understatement – is the foundation of one of the megastars of rock music. But certain things about his lifestyle don't always sit comfortably with a mainstream approach to Christian morality.

Now here is the crunch. How would you feel about an avowedly Christian development agency, passionate about addressing the issue of HIV/AIDS, joining hands with that rock star's foundation to fight the virus, knowing they could achieve far more together than they could do apart?

Dig deep beyond your panicky reflexes for a moment and ask an honest 'why not?' What do the poor need? What won't be done if the church soldiers on forever blinkered and only ever working with those who share its hopefully pristine and sanitised view of life?

As you are thinking, reflect on a church I read of recently by the name of St Sexburger's. They decided it would be best not to use the name of their church in the url for their web site 'in case it attracted the wrong kind of people'. In other words, 'let's not go inconveniencing a bunch of perverts who might bump into something pure and nice and so be offended'. Or more likely they had a sense that, with every click, such visitors would suck some of their blissful purity out of them, leaving them somewhat tarnished and compromised.

Is it this kind of subconscious attitude that permeates our approach to bringing poverty to an end? Far better to keep ourselves squeaky clean. To keep our distance from those we may not fully understand or some that have question marks over them. After all, we don't want our Christian-ness to get a bit soiled – no matter how good the reason – do we!

Now consider an actual example of this principle in another environment. The need to confront HIV/AIDS in a highly rural African culture, where the key players to help bring change are the Sangoma – a blend of witchdoctor, rune shaker and mystic. As the spiritual gatekeepers in many villages, the Sangoma are the people who have the ears of their community. So what are you going to do?

It is at this point that a clear commitment to following Jesus becomes highly relevant. As is confidence in the answer to that first question I asked you – that God is truly big enough for the church. Which is how it was for a group of Christian development workers faced with this very situation. Their answer was to take the side of the poor and to be convinced it involved no compromise to work with those who had a very different worldview and even a commitment to a very different power to their own.

And when they did, something very remarkable happened. A face-to-face meeting to create a common strategy had hardly started when a key player on the 'other side' began to show signs of being possessed by unclean spirits. They had to be escorted from the room – with everyone knowing what had happened and the explanation being given afterwards that, 'The spirits were telling her they were uncomfortable in your presence'.

This story reached me from someone who was actually there, who explained, 'What the Sangoma experienced was the reality of the two worlds. And they knew they had lost their authority in our presence.'

Far from becoming tarnished, the Christians had had an exactly opposite effect. 'What may all too easily sound like compromise was the very opposite,' explained my eyewitness. 'It was only because we were not willing to make concessions over who we were and what we stood for that we could be confident.'

And he added, 'In situations like this, whether the contrast between our convictions and attitudes and theirs are major or minor, our starting point should always be the conviction that they cannot be in our presence without feeling the effect of our God.'

God big enough for the church? Of course – as he was in this African setting. The church big enough for the needs of the poor? Of course not. But by having the right perspective, and allowing God to be our strength and guide, we can be the most significant part of the solution to world need.

And unless that's the role we take, we will be falling far short of our calling to be the church. And leaving millions to remain in poverty as a result.

40 Putting life into perspective

Where the words come from I don't know. And I can't vouch for every statistic quoted. But the sentiment is powerful.

Next time you – or someone nearby – are having a bad day try this for size.

'If you woke up this morning with more health than illness, you are more blessed than the million who will not survive this week.

'If you have never experienced the danger of battle, the loneliness of imprisonment, the agony of torture or the pangs of starvation, you are ahead of 500 million people in the world.

'If you can attend a church meeting without fear of harassment, arrest, torture or death, you are luckier than three billion people in the world.

'If you have food in the refrigerator, clothes on your back, a roof over your head and a place to sleep, you are richer than 75 per cent of the world.

'If you have money in the bank, in your purse and spare change in a dish somewhere, you are among the top eight per cent of the world's wealthy.'

These words may not exactly be 'Footprints' but they still speak volumes to us in our 'life must be perfect for me' world. Because for most people life is anything other than perfect.

When I first came across these words they'd been sent to someone for whom life was going considerably pear shaped. And they concluded with, '*And by reading this message you are doubly blessed because I was thinking about you and love you.*'

And isn't that the rub? It's not just that we can become so focused on our own needs that we fail to see them in their true perspective. It's that, in the process, we become distracted from thinking about – and genuinely loving – those who really know how bad things can be.

Two shopping lists

What it would cost to
- Help the world to feed itself – $8 billion
- Provide the world with clean water – $9 billion
- Provide universal primary education – $6 billion

What the world already spends
- On the military – $780 billion
- On illegal drugs – $400 billion
- On perfumes – $12 billion

41 Looking for Jesus in Bangkok

My taxi spluttered towards a slum area on the outskirts of Bangkok. And one question was foremost in my mind. Where, I wondered, would I see Jesus?

Six months into my role as Head of Church Action at World Vision UK I had absorbed the theory, that at the heart of everything this Christian development agency does is a commitment to long-term programmes 'owned' by the poor community themselves. And that these Area Development Projects (ADPs) give people the dignity of contributing to their own future, rather than endless hand outs and a series of 'quick fixes'.

But it was not so much the quality of the work I was interested in but its specifically Christian dimension. I wanted to see what it meant to be a 'Christian development agency' rather than a missionary or evangelistic one.

Where, I wondered, would witness to Jesus Christ be evident in the ADP I was about to visit? Particularly in a Buddhist nation where many are like the Thai taxi driver who jabbered 'Buddha is king' at me – while waving the New Testament, explaining that thirteen was his lucky number and what frightened him most was the Mafia.

So where would I see Jesus? It didn't take long.

My guide – and sharing the taxi – was Jeeranan Ratanadaranan from World Vision Thailand's national office. Arriving earlier than expected at the Pakhanong ADP I surveyed the simple but adequate office. And puzzled over the red drum kit sitting incongruously in one corner.

We were soon joined by the Project's Manager, the calm and capable Kannika Mahaphon. She began by walking me through a 'tour' of the Project's history – aided by a series of photographic montages. They'd taken time to identify the community leaders, and then built trust and given them a voice for their dreams.

And that was when I 'saw' Jesus – walking alongside them rather than invading and confronting. Allowing them to take the initiative and to have the responsibility for their own future.

History lesson over, we go visiting. First to the child day-care centre – identified by the community as a priority so mothers could work, adding to their household's meagre income.

Then to the slum homes, built over what seemed like a swamp – with basic facilities and little else. It's hard to believe people pay rent to live like this.

The Project is funded through child sponsorship. And it's from these slum homes the sponsored children come. 'Each home is visited by a church pastor,' explained Kannika, 'to make it clear how child sponsorship works and answer their questions.'

And here was Jesus again. The One who loved to engage in conversations that sprang from the questions people were provoked to ask. It's a model strewn through the book of Acts – and at the heart of World

Vision's Christian witness strategy. To live lives and do deeds that cause people to long to know 'why?'

In the Project the 'answers' include an invitation for adults to be part of a cell group and children to join a Sunday School in a house.

Next stop the Women's Co-operative – where a team of women are building their own small business making clothes and handicrafts. All made possible through a grant and training in machining and marketing.

The building is a fragile, makeshift 'hut'. And the women positively glow as Kannika explains they have nearly saved enough to gain a matching grant from the local authority to purchase a new workshop.

Finally to the school where 600 of the 700 pupils are sponsored children served by the Project. Without the help being given they would go hungry. Instead, thanks to their amazing Luncheon Club, they eat their fill.

In the school grounds they are growing vegetables and raising fish, edible frogs and chickens. The children do most of the work. World Vision funds a helper to make it happen.

And more questions are provoked as to why?

Jeeranan and Kannika mention lunch – and I hope this doesn't mean joining the queue for frogs. It doesn't. In a 'nicer part of town' they respond to my own questions.

Jeeranan's passion for the poor had come from a spell with Youth with a Mission. Her prayer, 'If you can use me as your instrument please do it' was being answered before my eyes. Kannika is working on an MA in Divinity at the local Baptist Seminary.

In my early days at World Vision I'd tried to identify their overtly Christian programmes. Now I know better.

Being Christian, for a Christian development agency, is not about bolted-on activities. It is deeply ingrained in the work they do, the approach they take and in the lives of their people. Like these two.

And those drums? Left over from a youth camp the local church had run for those wanting to know more. And many did.

They had seen Jesus – and so had I.

42 It's not hand outs kids want

Bring together children and stones and most likely you start thinking about damage. Considerable damage! But instead, think 'development'. With the children being asked for their views – positive or negative – of the way a development programme has impacted their community.

Using a simple technique, the children each arrange their ten stones on a grid to indicate the way they see change having happened over their access to education, their health, gender issues, the impact of hunger and so on. And then they do the same to help express what they see as their priorities for the future.

Care will be taken to build checks into the process due to the way children's memories of events can differ. Nevertheless, their views are to be treated as invaluable to the whole process.

What is going on in this simple rural scene? It is a development agency taking seriously what the United Nations have to say about children and what Jesus said and did a couple of thousand years or so earlier. Both would have us know that children are special and must to be treated that way.

The UN expresses it in their Convention on the Rights of the Child. It enshrines every child's right to freedom of expression and the right to be involved in matters that affect them if they wish. As for Jesus, it only takes a quick romp though the Gospels to capture the dignity he gave them and the importance he placed on them.

So the challenge when working with the poor is to make sure children are active participants in shaping their own future. To recognise they can often bring fresh insights into the issues that affect them. And that it's not just adults who have an inside track on things like health, education or more specifically sexual abuse, violence and war.

Does that sound too much like politically correct gobbledygook? Then please think again. Two years of research by World Vision on the issue of ending abuse, violence, and exploitation among children tells a different story. That violence is significantly reduced where children are directly involved in creating strategies designed to stop it happening or protect them when it does.

Why? Because, with their innocent, uncluttered and non-political minds, children often get to the heart of the matter more effectively than adults in the same environment. Which helps explain why a major recommendation of the survey was to '*Invite children to be full participants in establishing measures that offer protection, foster development and guarantee human rights.*'

Of course, such involvement must be fun and has to take on board their particular interests and stage of development. But with this in mind, good development practice involves helping children play a genuine role in the planning and implementation of programmes that will change their future. Like the example of the stones exercise, which is but one example among many. And to give you the full flavour, here come a whole load more.

In Sri Lanka 'Child Societies' teach organisational skills and the principles of democracy to their members. In the context of World Vision development programmes children learn how to budget as a group, about election processes and leadership skills. They are helped to identify the issues impacting them most and to work out their response. On the way they gain a greater confidence to speak in public. And hidden talents come bursting forth.

In Colombia, where civil war's been raging for half a century, children are training as agents of peace through the 'National Movement of Children for Peace'. This gives children insight into issues they face like loneliness, low self-esteem, rape, violence and drug/alcohol abuse. And to make the best kind of responses.

In the Philippines, 550 village children's groups are encouraged to develop their full potential in leadership. Annual assemblies take place in all 12 provinces – with children presenting issues and resolutions. The local government then responds, introducing laws and creating programmes. It's the work of a coalition of four development agencies, with World Vision taking the lead. And you'll find a similar story in places as widely spread as Tanzania, El Salvador, South Korea, Guatemala and Mexico.

Does it have an impact? Let fifteen-year-old Elia Munambala, the Vice-Chair for Tanzania's Junior Council have his say: '*This is crucial to nurturing our inherent optimism and preparing us for a constructive and meaningful adulthood.*' That may sound like a quote he prepared earlier but the sentiment is solid.

And so the story goes on. Those who are the future are helping create the future. Which is exactly how it should be.

43 Donors – the goose or the golden egg?

There's a well-worn euphemism in the charity world – where the un-PC 'fundraising' often becomes the much nicer sounding and far less in your face 'donor development'. If you are going to do some very dirty work it should at least sound benevolent.

After all, on the one hand we have poor communities – needing to be developed. And on the other the 'rich' – needing to have as much money extracted from them as possible to help it happen. That's the way 'fundraising' or its more sanitised euphemism 'donor development' is supposed to work. Isn't it?

The donor is simply an impersonal economic unit. A living and breathing hole in the wall machine. To be plundered for their wealth – though ever so politely. Evaluated on the basis of the size of their assets and their willingness to be separated from them. It is not exactly the end justifying the means, but close to it.

Sadly, that is all too often how fundraising works – no matter what it is called. But surely it really should be 'donor development'. Really. Really. Not least when those doing the extracting are themselves in the development business – with poor communities.

Those who are 'rich' are just as much made in the image of God as those who are 'poor'. Just as deserving of being treated as though this is true. Equally owning the right to a journey towards personal wholeness. If the poor are never to be mere objects of pity then those who have the financial means to contribute to them having a better future must never be treated as objects either.

That's why – however sincerely they may be done – tin rattling and door-to-door envelope collecting leave me feeling uncomfortable. They give the donor little opportunity to engage with either the issue or the eventual beneficiary. And leaves behind the understanding that what needs to be done has been done.

It's also why approaches like Child Sponsorship seem to offer so much more – because they do the very opposite, engaging the donor and taking them on a journey of discovery and involvement that leads to their own development.

But it is more than the method that matters. The issue is the underlying attitude, which then breaks forth into actions. And it's here things get a bit spooky. Because I find someone else has been thinking my thoughts – and expressing them far more clearly than I ever could.

Larry F. Johnston is a fundraising guru with some thirty years' experience at the highest level with Christian agencies in the US. In essence he puts the issue this way: that all people are 'more than human beings, we are human *becomings* with extraordinary potential'. And with those who are Christians 'destined to become conformed to the image of Christ'.

With that as his backdrop, Larry calls for an approach to fundraising based on the 'transformational development' of the donor, instead of what he calls Transactional Fundraising – or what I call 'grab the money and run'.

For him (us!) those in the business of extracting money should be 'first and foremost people developers'. With the process involved seen as 'not merely something done to support ministry, it is ministry'.

Larry has created an extensive list of highly telling comparisons between the traditional 'Transactional Fundraising' (the grab the money stuff) and Transformational Development (the let's treat the donor as human stuff). Try this sample for size – and give him the credit as you read.

Transactional Fundraising (TF) sees the *Donor as Object* – with donors viewed less as individuals with their own hopes, dreams, and aspirations, and more as walking chequebooks. In contrast, Transformational Development (TD) has the *Donor as Subject* – viewed as co-journeyers with a 'voice' that needs to be recognised, honoured, and affirmed.

TF is about the *Golden Egg* – with a focus on what the donor can cough up for you. TD is about *The Goose* – the living being who, if sufficiently cared for, makes possible a lifetime of golden eggs.

TF is about *solicitation* – plucking the goose so as to get the least amount of hissing. And TD about *cultivation/ appreciation* – seeing solicitation as merely one key point in a continuous process of cultivation, appreciation, affirmation, and so on.

TF is *one-dimensional* – seeing fundraising as about money and nothing else. TD is *multi-dimensional* – about people, prayer, integrity, trust, relationships, values, faith, hopes, dreams, vision, mission, programmes, and a whole lot more.

TF is *temporal* – the focus only on the here and now. And TD is *eternal* – seeing all things – even small things like a cup of cold water given in Christ's name – in the perspective of eternity. And behaving that way.

So dance on through today's world of euphemisms – where, for example, 'liar' now reads 'economical with the truth'. And when you read 'donor development' rather than 'fundraising' pray to God that this is really what is happening.

For more on Larry F. Johnston's insights visit www.mcconkey-johnston.com.

44 If only we could clone people like this

By reading this far you have encountered a lot about sharp thinking, wise methodology, and right approach. But you know all too well that technique alone is never going to be the answer when it comes to working with the poor. Because, ultimately, the most important ingredient is the right kind of people.

For example, take the young American pastor holding a Korean orphan child in his arms and weeping. His name is Bob Pierce. The scene is the Korean War of the early 1950s. Within days he will back in his homeland telling the story of the need of so many like the one he is holding, raising money and support to make a difference.

The Asian bloodbath left some five million people dead. And, in South Korea alone, was responsible for an estimated 200,000 orphans, 600,000 widows, and five million refugees. Bob Pierce was to write: '*People ate raw sweet potatoes dug from the fields or went hungry. Women died along the road as they tried to escape the falling bombs.*

Homeless children sat by the roadside and cried in helpless-
ness. Sometimes they stole. Other times they held out a tin can
crying "Pap chusiyo" [rice please]. I was there and saw the
misery - this was war, a war that was to produce a generation
of orphans.'

Faced with human tragedy on that scale, Bob Pierce
realised that what did no more than move him actually
broke God's heart. Bob was to make his prayer '*Let my*
heart be broken with the things that break the heart of God'.
And God answered his prayers.

Over the next half a century Bob's passion and dedication was to be the foundation for what has become one
of the largest agencies working with the poor in the
world – World Vision. It was his response to a world of
need that directly led to almost all the stories illustrating
this book and many more beside. More than that, Bob
Pierce was also to go on to found Samaritan's Purse,
another remarkable international agency working to
transform the lives of the poor.

Bob Pierce knew nothing of 'holistic and sustainable
development'. Or capacity building, micro-finance,
problem trees, the special plight of girls and those who
are handicapped. Or any of the rest of the rich thinking
that's the daily fare of those now at work to help change
the future of the poor, and which splashes over the pages
you have been reading. But he had passion. Passion to
pray 'God break my heart' and then the guts to put his
God-given compassion into action.

Having met Bob Pierce there are four more heroes I'd
like to introduce you to. Meet Thomson Chipeta, who
grew up as an orphan in Malawi. 'There was never any
money,' he would tell you. 'Instead of attending school, I
worked from a young age, putting learning for later in

life.' Yet through hard work and dedication Thomson became a Presbyterian minister, serving the church and its community for over forty years.

But between 1991 and 1992, two of Thomson's daughters died, leaving ten orphans between them. What had once been his experience had now become their experience. And so began a dream – to build a home for orphaned children. Something that only began in earnest in 1997 when Thomson retired from the church.

Today, take an hour's drive from Malawi's capital and then 15km through dense bush and trees on a gravel road to a small settlement. There you'll find the cluster of new buildings that make up the 'Home of Hope', a refuge and the promise of a future for 185 children, among them 36 babies. But it all came from small beginnings. The vision of an orphan. A patch of unpromising land given by the Presbyterian Church. And a 100 Kwacha donation – less than £10 – from a South African missionary.

But Thomson's faithful prayers were matched with hard work and sound financial management – and the miracle happened! His Home of Hope attracted interest from a local development agency, the European Union and even the German Embassy. But as much as the money they provided was needed, without the outstanding dedication of Reverend Chipeta, there would be no Home of Hope today for the orphaned children in Malawi.

And nor would Thomson be recognised as an outstanding example of how God-fearing Africans can bring African solutions to African problems. Visit the Home of Hope and you will sit with those who will one day be doctors, engineers, scientists, and more. And all because one man, with an unpromising beginning, in the later years of his life unconditionally shares his love with children and gives them hope.

Meet Manang Mars, whose life has been one tough melodrama. She's from a poor family in the Philippine village of Amungan – and the third of ten children. With pain Manang remembers her brothers and sisters being distributed to relatives because their parents could not afford to care for them. She was fortunate to be sent to school by relatives. Later, she worked in a bakeshop owned by a kind couple who saw her potential and let her study a six-month bookkeeping course.

Today, Manang will tell you, 'I have a simple dream – to give back God's blessing.' Visit her and you will be made welcome in her humble house of bamboo walls and tin roof. It has changed little since it was built few decades ago. And she dreams of nothing bigger or better. For Manang, life is not about getting but sharing – especially with children.

Her story reaches back over thirty years – to the point when World Vision began a development programme in her village. Two of her children became sponsored children and she became a volunteer. Eventually she was asked to handle the bookkeeping at the project on a temporary basis. Hesitant, she then figured if some of the first followers of Jesus never had much of an education but were able to serve people, she could too!

Her dedication was quickly recognised – and she became the project's official bookkeeper with a salary as well. She threw herself headlong into the job. Next she was assigned as community development worker for six villages served by the project – working closely with 685 sponsored children.

People around her speak of Manang's dedication. Her house has become a meeting place for the project. Children come to her any time of day. Staff and sponsored families with problems seek her out for advice and comfort. She believes, though she is poor, God created her to do something for humankind. 'Ayokong mabuhay sa sarili (I don't want to live just for myself).'

And Manang Mars' work is not over yet. With her children having finished school and pursuing their own careers, she dreams of using her humble resources – and those of her now working children – to help more poor children in the community. For, to her, this is what life is truly all about.

Meet Charles Mully whose story begins with the theft of his car from a Nairobi street over twenty years ago. Despite the poverty of his childhood, Charles was a highly successful businessman. Having driven to Kenya's capital he ignored the advice of some street children offering to show him a vacant parking space in exchange for a little money. And never saw his car again.

But what troubled Charles Mully most was not the loss of his vehicle but the plight of the street children. They reminded him of his own early life; of the poverty, hunger and suffering he had personally experienced during his own childhood. And, with his wife Esther, he asked God what they should do for street children – despite having eight children of their own to care for.

As a first step, Charles and Esther opened their home to street children willing to live there. It started with just three, who then persuaded more to abandon life on the streets for a better life in Charles Mully's house. Soon the house was full. Which meant there was another decision to make.

Through hard work and enterprise, Charles had come to own a chain of businesses – including a prosperous insurance agency, a petroleum products distribution firm, a security company, a shop and a public transport company. His conclusion? That, to concentrate on caring for street children, he would sell the lot, with some of the proceeds going to extending the premises and so establishing the Mully Children's Family Home.

Besides food, accommodation and healthcare, the former street children learned to read and write. Older children learned carpentry, tailoring and dressmaking, metal work and masonry to equip them to stand on their own feet.

Today, with the additional financial support of World Vision, there are 120 children in the original Mully Children's Family Home. And a 'sister' home on Charles Mully's 40-acre farm six hours' drive away cares for 330 more. Visit and you'll easily spot the strong family bond among the children. As Charles and Esther walk around the compound you'll hear shouts of 'Dad!' and 'Mum!' Because that's exactly what they have become.

Meet Armelea Aketch, at fifty a small-scale businesswoman who is a fishmonger at her local Korogocho market in one of the slum districts of Nairobi. She's a woman with a heart of gold. When Armelea's neighbours lost their lives to the HIV/AIDS scourge, leaving five desperate children aged seven months to fourteen years' she felt compelled to help.

'Knowing these children had no hope my conscience compelled me to welcome them into my home,' says Armelea, a widow herself with three children of her own to care for. She adds that, as a Christian, she knew God was testing her faith. 'Children are God's gift to all of us and we have to care for them, whether they are ours or not,' she adds.

Four heroes. Five if you include Bob Pierce – and we should. Five about whom you may well think 'if only it was possible to clone people like this'. But that's not God's way. He doesn't create replicas. Only originals. Each of us is distinct and special – with the freedom to become all that God intends and to live the way he longs for us to do.

So the issue is not one of sending in the clones. But for a multitude of people who will work with the poor God's way, putting as much rich thinking into action as they can. But all the while doing so with hearts broken as God's is broken.

Could you pray that prayer with me? 'Let my heart be broken with the things that break the heart of God.' Please God make it so – because thinking doesn't get any richer than that.

Digging a little deeper

Interested in exploring more deeply some of the issues covered by this book? Then here are some suggestions for further reading.

Faith in Development – Belshaw, D., R. Calderisi and C. Sugden, eds. (2001), Oxford: Regnum

The God of the Poor – Hughes, Dewi (1998), Carlisle: OM Publishing

Beyond the Good Samaritan – Morisy, Ann (1997), London: Mowbray

Walking with the Poor Myers – Bryant (1999), New York: Orbis

Mission as Transformation – Samuel, Vinay and Christ Sugden, eds. (1999), Oxford Regnum

Being Human, Being Church – Warren, Robert (1995), London: HarperCollins

Seeing the World Through God's Eyes – Williams, Derek (2002), Milton Keynes: World Vision

A word about World Vision

This book draws deeply on the experience and practice of World Vision, the international development and aid agency dedicated to relieving suffering and improving the quality of life of the world's poorest people.

World Vision is a Christian organisation with a commitment founded on Jesus Christ – whose life demonstrated compassion and service to all, which is why World Vision helps people no matter what their religious beliefs may be.

World Vision UK is one of some ninety national, self-governing, World Vision offices. The worldwide staff numbers about 12,000, of whom around 97 per cent are nationals.

World Vision UK has a simple manifesto:

'We will not rest until every child, in every part of the world, enjoys the right to life, dignity, justice and hope. So they can fulfil their God-given potential and, one day, see their own children grow up to experience the same.'

The heart of World Vision's work is long-term development programmes with communities of as many as 60,000 people. These programmes deal with all the issues that represent poverty – health, clean water, education, food, job creation and so on. And also address the complex relationships between them.

These programmes are funded mainly though Child Sponsorship, with the donations pooled so the whole community can benefit as well as the sponsored child.

As a Christian agency, World Vision provides special resources for churches and their members. These include:

Churches in Partnership – through which a church can make a long-term commitment to a poor community as they journey towards standing on their own feet.

Gifts for Life – a way for a church to provide a significant resource for a poor community, from a water well to an ox and cart.

The Alternative Christmas Card – ending the annual Christmas card scrum for churches through one card they all sign, with the money saved going to help poor communities.

The 24-hour Famine – an annual youth initiative where teens raise sponsorship to go hungry for a day.

WorldView – a free email newsletter on 'God and the poor' sent out fortnightly.

Harvest and Christmas resources – to help churches celebrate and support the poor.

Because – a three-times-a-year mini-mag sharing the Christian heart of World Vision.

Prayer Guide – a bi-monthly guide to praying for the world's poor.

For details log on to www.worldvision.org.uk/church or phone 0800 50 10 10.

Equipping Christians to live actively, biblically and wholeheartedly for Christ — that's the goal of all that Spring Harvest does.

The Main Event

The largest Christian event of its kind in Europe — an Easter-time gathering of over 60,000 people for learning, worship and fun. The programme includes varied and inspiring choices for everyone, no matter how old or young, and no matter where you are in your Christian life.

Resources

- *Books* to help you understand issues that matter — prayer, family issues, Bible themes, workplace and more
- *Music albums* introducing new songs and showcasing live worship from the Main Event each year
- *Childrens resources* including popular music albums and songbooks
- *Songbooks* to introduce the best new worship material each year
- *Audio tapes* of teaching from Spring Harvest — a selection of thousands is available to choose from
- *Youth pastoral resources, songwords projection software, video services and more...*

Conferences

- *Youthwork the conference* — for volunteer youth workers, run in partnership with Youthwork magazine, YFC, Oasis Youth Action and the Salvation Army

- *At Work Together* to equip workers to effectively live and witness for Christ in today's challenging workplace.

Le Pas Opton is a beautiful four star holiday site on the French Vendée coast, exclusively owned and operated by Spring Harvest. Mobile homes, tents or your own tent/tourer — take your choice at this delightful resort where you'll find top quality facilities and excellent service.

Our aim at *Le Pas Opton* is to give you the opportunity for relaxation and refreshment of body, mind and spirit. Call Spring Harvest Holidays on 0870 060 3322 for a free brochure.

INVESTOR IN PEOPLE

For more information contact our Customer Service team on 01825 769000 or visit our website at www.springharvest.org

Spring Harvest. A Registered Charity.